332.452   Sennholz
S478g   Gold is money

DATE DUE	BORROWER'S NAME	NUMBER
NOV 1	Neal Frey	fac
	6/14/78 10/4/79	
APR 3 0	Michele Allgier	
MAY 2 3	C. Buffington	

GOLD IS MONEY

CONTRIBUTIONS IN ECOMONICS
AND ECONOMIC HISTORY

American Financing of World War I
Charles Gilbert

The Depression of the Nineties: An Economic History
Charles Hoffmann

Paternalism and Protest: Southern Cotton Mill Workers and Organized Labor, 1875-1905
Melton Alonza McLaurin

Business and Politics in America from the Age of Jackson to the Civil War: The Career Biography of W. W. Corcoran
Henry Cohen

Business Depressions and Financial Panics: Essays in American Business and Economic History
Samuel Rezneck

Towards an Integrated Society: Reflections on Planning, Social Policy and Rural Institutions in India
Tarlok Singh

The Age of Giant Corporations: A Microeconomic History of American Business, 1914-1970
Robert Sobel

Samuel Gompers and the Origins of the American Federation of Labor, 1848-1896
Stuart Bruce Kaufman

Statistical View of the Trusts: A Manual of Large American Industrial and Mining Corporations Active around 1900
David Bunting

State and Regional Patterns in American Manufacturing, 1860-1900
Albert W. Niemi, Jr.

The American Banking Community and New Deal Banking Reforms, 1933-1935
Helen M. Burns

GOLD
I$
MONEY

Edited with an Introduction by

Hans F. Sennholz

Contributions in Economics
and
Economic History, Number 12

GREENWOOD PRESS

Westport, Connecticut • London, England

Library of Congress Cataloging in Publication Data

Sennholz, Hans F
     Gold is money.

     (Contributions in economics and economic history ; no. 12)
     Includes bibliographical references and index.
     1. Gold standard. 2. Monetary policy. I. Title.
HG297.S44   332.4'5   74-15161
ISBN 0-8371-7804-5

Library of Congress Catalog Card Number: 74-15161
ISBN: 0-8371-7804-5

First published in 1975

Greenwood Press, a division of Williamhouse-Regency Inc.
51 Riverside Avenue, Westport, Connecticut 06880

Manufactured in the United States of America

CONTENTS

Introduction

With the breakdown of the international monetary order in August 1971, the world entered a new phase in international finance and commerce. For some twenty-seven years, since the Bretton Woods Agreement, the U.S. dollar had been the most important currency to which the free world monetary system was safely anchored. But the American suspension of gold payments on August 15, 1971, the dollar devaluations in December 1971 and February 1973, followed by sinking floats in the foreign exchange markets, have lifted the dollar anchor and cast adrift the international monetary order.

Prospects for creating a more stable system appear remote. True, some optimists still cling to the hope that the system can be overhauled in a year or two. They place their confidence in a special committee of the International Monetary Fund's board of governors, the "Group of Twenty," of which eleven are from industrial countries and nine from less developed areas. But the frequent consultations and meetings of the group clearly reveal that it is most difficult to reach agreement. The differences in attitude and viewpoint among governments are considerable and the great diversity of national positions and interests is discouraging.

The official U.S. position as expressed by former Treasury Secretary George Shultz emphasizes the need for frequent exchange rate adjustments in order to correct balance-of-payments imbalances. Sound international trade and finance can be achieved either through a system of floating exchange rates involving some occasional official intervention, or exchange parities subject to frequent and relatively small adjustments. Such a system, according to the U.S. view, should be supported by the convertibility of national currencies into reserve assets that serve a common denominator or numéraire for currencies. Of course, these assets must be made to grow in order to facilitate expansion of international trade and investment. They must be created periodically in the necessary amounts. In fact, the United States would like to make Special Drawing Rights (SDRs) the principal medium of international reserves. They should cease to be partly repayable in gold, their guarantees in gold should be eliminated, and the limits beyond which the creditor countries are not obliged to accept SDRs in settlement of debtors' deficits should be lifted.

On the other hand, the creditor countries quickly point out that any addition of SDRs and the removal of those safeguards would render the international monetary order even more inflationary. Financing of persistent deficits by SDRs would tend to undermine and ultimately destroy the arrangement. After all, they ask, how long can creditor countries be expected to finance the chronic deficits of debtors?

And finally, there are the less developed countries who would like to link the creation of SDRs to economic aid by the advanced countries. Why, they are asking, should SDRs, for the most part, be given to the United States and other industrial countries? Why should they not be used to finance capital improvements and alleviate the poverty of the world?

All governments seem to agree that the importance of gold as international money should be gradually reduced. The U.S. government whose holdings declined from a record high of $26.9 billion in August 1949 to some $10 billion in 1971 is especially eager to reduce the role of gold. The European countries and Japan, who quadrupled their gold reserves over the same period and now are holding more than $23 billion, basically agree with the U.S. position but wonder about the alternative: U.S. dollars or SDR. With nearly 1,000 full or partial devaluations of national currencies since the end of World War II how can any one currency issued by a government or association of governments be trusted to serve as international money?

There cannot be any doubt that the world's monetary system is changing rapidly. The swift course of recent events clearly indicates that a major change is under way. But what is the direction of this change? Will it be a patchwork of symptom remedies that are mere reactions to emerging crises, and as such will fragment the international financial and economic order? Indeed, the danger of such reforms is imminent and profound. How can the monetary authorities that created the present disorder be expected to bring order and stability to the world? Accelerating inflation all over the globe and frequent upheavals in the exchange markets are strengthening inflationary expectations. We are now observing the first indications of a worldwide flight out of money. Since the U.S. dollar no longer affords a relatively safe monetary haven, and stringent controls keep investors from access to some stronger European currencies, an international flight into "real values" is developing. The demand for land, housing, and other durable goods, collector's items and, above all, gold, is growing.

Whoever ventures to speak kindly of gold or the gold standard places his good name and professional reputation in great jeopardy. For the number of friends of gold has dwindled to a tiny remnant whose voice is easily lost in the noise of popular monetary discussion. After all, most contemporary economists adhere to the monetary orthodoxy of our time which makes government the creator and guardian of the people's money. They are dedicated to fiat issues that permit government regulation and that manipulate and afford flexibility for the sake of central planning. In the name of social progress, money and credit are managed by central authorities, and the unmanageable gold is decried as a barbaric metal, a relic of the past.

This book summarily rejects this statist orthodoxy. Its nine writers are in full agreement that money is not the product of a legislative act, but the inevitable result of man's division of labor and exchange economy. Wherever enterprising men seek to exchange their goods and services for more marketable goods that facilitate further exchanges for other goods, the precious metals, especially gold, are most suited to serve as money. The writers are aware that for some 2,500 years small pieces of gold and silver, called coins, constituted universal money. It survived two millennia in spite of countless attempts by hosts of governments to manipulate it or replace it with their own media. They are convinced that gold will soon return as universal money and prevail long after the present rash of national fiats is forgotten or relegated to currency museums.

The essays of this collection are the product of a lecture series given at Grove City College during the 1973 Spring Semester. Without an editor's blueprint each contributor chose his own object of analysis. The only plan that helped to give structure and content to this collection is visible in the editor's selection of the contributors. As economists, historians, jurists, philosophers, or theologians they all are members of the gold standard remnant and are the courageous advocates of the coming monetary order.

We are grateful to the Philip M. McKenna Foundation whose generous assistance made our work possible. May it contribute to the memory of Philip McKenna, a great American and member of the remnant.

H.F.S.

GOLD IS MONEY

1

The Plight of the Dollar

G. C. WIEGAND

Professor of Economics, Southern Illinois University

"The dollar is as good as gold," announced the Bretton Woods Agreement, and for twenty-five years the dollar passed freely as the most widely used international medium of exchange. But while the world accepted the dollar in place of gold, its inner strength deteriorated slowly until it was devalued twice in 1971 and again in 1973, and was no longer freely acceptable. What are the reasons for the debacle?

There are two possible explanations. The weakness of the dollar may be the result of temporary international causes —America's heavy military expenditures abroad, and the failure of the American economy to adjust quickly to the economic recovery of war-torn Europe and Asia. These temporary causes can be overcome through emergency measures and "international cooperation." According to the

3

other explanation, the plight of the dollar is the result of fundamental disequilibria within the American economy which cannot be eliminated through "international coopera-tion" and dollar devaluations. The former was the official view of the United States, and most of the world, during the 1960s and early 1970s, despite growing evidence to the contrary. The latter view is set forth in this essay.

Foreign exchange rates do not exist in a vacuum, and the flow of international funds in the long run is not controlled by "speculators," although large-scale hedging operations and sudden movements of flight capital can, temporarily, turn a basic disequilibrium into a sudden crisis. Just as the balance of payments, foreign exchange rates constitute a barometer of whether the economy and the prevailing price structure of a nation are more or less in equilibrium with the rest of the world. This international equilibrium in turn requires that the national economic structure not be too far out of balance. The chronic weakness of the dollar stems from the fact that for twenty years the United States has increased the supply of paper dollars more rapidly than the supply of goods and services, and, as a nation, has consumed too much—in the private as well as the public sector—and has not invested enough, until the American economy can no longer fully com-pete in world markets. The plight of the dollar can be cured only by eliminating the fundamental socioeconomic dis-equilibria within the American economy which produce the chronic overconsumption.

For more than two decades, Washington and the rest of the world treated the American balance-of-payments deficit first as a curiosity and then as a minor problem which could be handled through ad hoc emergency measures rather than major policy changes.[1] By the time it became obvious, during the latter part of the 1960s, that the weakness of the dollar was the result of fundamental disequilibria within the American economy, Washington was too preoccupied with the Vietnam conflict and domestic social tensions to undertake the potentially politically dangerous economic reforms necessary to reinforce the dollar. The surplus nations, meanwhile, out of loyalty to the United States and to the Bretton Woods system (or, more likely, because they feared the possibility of a monetary collapse) continued to support the steadily weakening dollar often at great cost to their own economies. Thus, a possibly fateful decade was lost, during which the dollar and the international monetary system of the free world could have been restored relatively easily to a sound basis.

OVERSPENDING AND OVERCONSUMPTION

The progressive weakening of the dollar, resulting in the virtual abandonment of the basic assumptions of the Bretton Woods system, is the direct result of the widespread notion that a government can assure lasting prosperity and an ever rising standard of living by creating enough purchasing power through deficit spending and easy credit. Throughout the 1950s and 1960s, the artificially inflated demand increased faster than the supply of goods and services, and the American people consumed more than the American economy could produce under existing social and political restraints.

The excess consumption was made possible through increased reliance on foreign resources, resulting in the chronic balance-of-payments deficits, and through inadequate capital formation in the widest sense. America consumed too much, domestic as well as foreign goods, and saved too little, which over the course of years undermined the ability of large segments of the American economy to satisfy the expanded demand at home at competitive prices and to meet foreign competition in world markets. America acted like the man who enjoyed life, while neglecting to maintain his house, until, after a few years, the roof began to leak.

The decay of the inner cities and of the railroads; the "energy crisis" which had been building up for years; the shortage of lumber resulting from the lack of industrial capacity to process

the available timber; the growing inability of large segments of
the economy to hold their own in world markets—these are all
reflections of the inadequate capital formation during the
1950s and 1960s.

Man-hour productivity depends upon machinery and the
necessary infrastructure, and if capital formation is inadequate, productivity increases too slowly. During the 1960s
man-hour productivity in America grew by 35 percent, compared with 188 percent in Japan, 87 percent in Germany, and
75 percent in France.[2] Productivity grew more slowly in
America than in virtually all industrialized nations, and in
almost every year U.S. wages and fringe benefits increased
more rapidly than productivity, thus raising unit cost and
pushing up prices in general.

The failure of the American economy to meet the inflated
demand must be understood in the widest sense. It is not
merely a question of an excess of imports over exports; the
problem extends to every aspect of America's economic, social,
and political life. High wages and high per unit cost are undoubtedly important factors in America's growing inability to
meet foreign competition, and the high unit cost in turn is
partly due, at least in some industries, to technological
obsolescence. The plight of the dollar, however, cannot be
attributed entirely to the fact that the American worker can no
longer compete with the lower paid foreign worker. Between
1970 and 1972, wages and prices rose far more rapidly in
Germany and Japan than in the United States, yet it was during
these years that the traditional American export surplus turned
into a large import surplus, and the dollar crisis became acute,
while the mark and the yen became pillars of strength.

In addition to the high wage scales, many other factors add to
the pressure on the dollar. High taxes, especially state and
local taxes, public waste, the attitude of labor, the ever growing government bureaucracy, and the threat of increasing
foreign exchange restrictions all affect, directly or indirectly,
the value of the dollar. Most important factor, however, is that

the inflation-fed consumption exceeds the production of goods and services. American exports and imports are affected more by the overall demand than by prices. Or, in the language of the economist, exports and imports are more income- than price-elastic. The cost of travel in Western Europe increased by 25 to 30 percent between 1970 and 1973, yet the total number of American tourists actually increased, because their disposable income in inflated dollars had increased by 25 percent during the same three years. Nor is the volume of exports primarily determined by prices. Between 1970 and 1972, American exports rose by about $6 1/2 billion or 13 percent, even though American prices (measured in terms of consumer prices) rose by 10 percent. Foreigners will buy sophisticated American machinery in preference to cheaper Japanese goods because they have more confidence in American workmanship, design, and especially service. They buy large American jets and computers, whatever their price, because they are produced only in America.

The plight of the dollar cannot be understood in strictly economic terms, especially not in terms of relative price levels. The attempt to "cheapen" the dollar through devaluations in order to lower the export price of American goods deals merely with the obvious rather than the more fundamental causes. Ultimately, the chronic deficit in the American balance of payments is but a reflection of fundamental cultural and social changes in America.

THE CHANGING MOOD IN AMERICA

Man's actions are determined by the ideas which he holds about himself, society, and the world in which he lives. During the past thirty to forty years, the American people have radically changed their outlook on life. In the 1930s, the great middle class still clung to the traditional social ethics of hard work, frugality, and profound distrust of government intervention. Since then, the pendulum has swung in the opposite direction. The great majority of the American people no longer see value in work itself. Work—a minimum of work at maximum pay—has become a means to an end: to enable all to enjoy an ever higher standard of living.

At the same time, as the will to produce declined, the desire to consume increased. We live in a "consumer culture," we are part of the "fun cult." Former Mayor Lindsay recently spoke of New York as the "fun city," even though more than 15 percent of its people are on relief—a percentage which was reached in ancient Rome in the third century, when the economic and social decay progressed rapidly.

The middle class of yesteryears built for the future. It was a social, if not a moral, obligation to increase the substance of the family from one generation to the next. As Keynes put it: "The duty of 'savings' became nine-tenths of virtue and the growth of the cake the object of a true religion . . . The virtue of the cake was that it was never to be consumed, neither by you nor by your children after you."[3] The difference between having a "cake" and not having one was the nineteenth-century difference between the middle class and the proletariat. As Keynes pointed out, the frugality of the middle class constituted an all-important economic asset during the nineteenth century, by providing the capital needed for industrialization.

But then came the great depression of the 1930s, and "oversaving" became an economic liability. The social virtue of yesteryears turned into a social vice, at least temporarily. In the mid-1930s, the Federal Reserve held almost $6 billion in excess member bank reserves, which would have been enough to enable the banking system to expand its credit by an amount almost equal to the total national debt. Obviously, this was a striking example of "oversaving."

Keynes' analysis was perfectly correct at the time the "General Theory" was published in 1936: the world suffered from oversaving and underconsumption. But this situation changed quickly with the outbreak of World War II three years later. Even before the United States entered the war, the excess reserves had declined by 40 percent, and ever since Pearl Harbor, consumption—"guns and/or butter"—has exceeded production in America and throughout the world.

Yet this obvious fact is disregarded by the politicians, the "experts," and the general public. During the 1930s, the world "oversaved" and since the 1940s the world has been "overconsuming." This is the simple explanation for the fact that between 1945 and 1972, the American dollar lost almost three-fourths of its domestic purchasing power,[4] and the various paper currencies throughout the world lost, on an average, over 85 percent of their value. Never in the history of mankind has there been such a drastic destruction of monetary values in such a short time. The intellectual and cultural convulsions throughout Western civilization are to a large extent a reflection of the loss of confidence in material, that is, monetary values. This loss of confidence in the future, this Keynesian "in the long run we are all dead" spirit, in turn, stimulates consumption and hampers investment. Let us live today. "D'après nous le déluge."

There are various ways in which capital formation can be measured. As far as the spirit of the time is concerned, the percentage of savings in relation to disposable income is probably most significant. Americans save 6 to 8 percent, the Germans 12 to 15 percent, and the Japanese 20 to 25 percent of their disposable income. To the extent that these savings are invested in the maintenance and expansion of productive capacity, instead of being used to finance the bureaucracy and the welfare state, man-hour productivity and the overall productivity of the nation increase. While Americans enjoyed an ever higher standard of living during the postwar decades because they consumed much and saved little, and since the 1960s spent an ever larger share of the Gross National Product (GNP) on the cradle-to-the-grave welfare state, the Germans and Japanese lived for years at a miserably low level, and saved and invested a very large share of their income. By the mid-1960s, the results became obvious: Germany and Japan, and less obviously other countries, began to outproduce the United States, a situation which in due course undermined the position of the dollar as the key currency of the free world.

The United States accounts for not quite 6 percent of the world's population. In the 1950s we produced and consumed about 37 percent of the world's goods and services. By the early 1970s, the percentage had declined to less than 25 percent. But America is still by far the richest and most productive country in the world, even though we no longer "earn our way."

A few figures will illustrate the trend. Between 1950 and 1960, during the "conservative" Truman and Eisenhower years, the output of goods and services, the GNP in fixed dollars, increased by 38 percent.[5] Federal spending, meanwhile grew from $40 billion to $94 billion, i.e., by 135 percent. Commercial Bank credit rose by 56 percent,[6] consumer credit by 180 percent,[7] and home mortgages by 213 percent.[8]

At the same time, the balance-of-payments deficit grew slowly but steadily.[9] The gold reserves declined from $24.5 billion at the end of 1949 to $19.5 billion ten years later—"a wholesome redistribution of international reserves" as some experts argued—while the foreign short-term obligations more than doubled, from $8.8 to $19.4 billion.

While private consumption, public spending, and credit increased far more rapidly during the 1950s than the production of goods and services, thus setting the stage for the great inflation of the 1960s, the Federal Reserve still pursued a fairly conservative policy. Federal Reserve credit increased by only 34 percent during the 1950s, less rapidly than the real GNP, and for all practical purposes at the end of the 1950s the dollar was still "as good as gold"—at least it was regarded as such throughout the world.

The mood of the country, moreover, was still essentially conservative. It resembled more that of the 1920s and 1930s than that of the 1960s. For the great middle class, Horatio Alger had not yet become a comical figure, and Puritan ethics were still respectable. To be sure, the goal of "full employment," that the federal government can and must provide every American with a suitable job, had been accepted by Congress, the White House, and the people. Only Utopians and social extremists thought that Washington could and should "abolish poverty."

And then, at a critical point in the nation's history, came the presidential campaign of 1960, with its violent charges and countercharges and the first serious "dollar crisis," for a short time the gold price in London rose to $42, equal to a depreciation of the dollar by about 20 percent. This was obviously a danger signal, especially since the gold reserves dropped sharply during 1960 from $19.5 to $17.8 billion, and short-term obligations rose from $19.4 to $21.4 billion. At least some people began to worry about the dollar, even though America's wealth and productive capacity were so great that the weakness of the dollar could readily be overcome, provided the American people and its leaders had the will to make the necessary sacrifices.

Instead, the country embarked upon the wildest inflationary spree in its history, reassured by the dictum of the experts that they could "fine-tune" the economy and assure maximum employment and growth, greater prosperity, without inflation. The Federal Reserve abandoned its relatively conservative policy of the 1950s, and the great mass of the people, fired by the promises of the politicians, came to believe that Washington could buy the millennium through the clever manipulation of paper dollars.

Between 1960 and 1972, GNP in real terms increased by almost 60 percent, or at an average of 5 percent, compared with a growth rate of 3.8 percent during the 1950s. At the same time, Federal Reserve credit jumped by 164 percent, more than 2 1/2 times as fast as the output of goods and services, and the money supply (currency, demand, and time deposits in commercial banks) increased by almost 145 percent. Federal spending rose from about $95 billion in fiscal 1960 to almost $232 in fiscal 1972, an increase of 144 percent, and inflation permeated every aspect of the economy. While the disposable income of the American consumer in depreciating dollars rose by 126 percent, consumer credit grew by 180 percent, and the mortgage debt by almost 145 percent. New car sales increased by 65 percent between 1960 and 1972, an important factor in the worsening pollution; consumption of electric power rose by almost 60 percent, which is one of the reasons for the growing "energy crisis." What had been regarded as luxuries in the 1950s—weekend houses, motor boats, swimming pools, and vacations in Europe—became part of the accepted standard of living of a wide segment of the middle class. Even the twenty-five million Americans who were classified as "poor" by the government experienced a rapid rise in their standard of living: they too had steaks, cars, TV sets, and greatly improved medical care.

By the beginning of the 1970s, the policy of chronic "mild" inflation was running into serious difficulties. Of the more than $300 billion of new money created between 1960 and 1972, at least $60 billion (some estimates run as high as $80 billion) flowed abroad in payment of goods, services, and assets which the American economy had failed to produce. These billions in due course formed the basis of the huge and volatile Eurodollar market. Gold reserves declined from $17.8 to $11 billion between 1960 and 1970, while short-term foreign obligations, still supposedly payable on demand in gold, rose from $21 to $47 billion. The dollar was manifestly no longer "as good as gold," and the stage was set for a major crisis.

During the 1960s, Washington had tried to camouflage the growing weakness of the dollar through a variety of emergency measures. The London gold pool maintained the price of gold at $35 an ounce, swap arrangements were used to counteract sudden runs on the dollar, while year after year new restrictions were placed on the outflow of dollars.[10]

The attempt to restrict the use of the New York capital market by foreign borrowers and by American multinational corporations backfired in an unexpected and dangerous fashion. Confronted with increasing restrictions in New York, the business shifted abroad, as American banks opened some 500 overseas branches,[11] and the Eurodollar market partly replaced the New York capital market. Since there are no reserve requirements for Eurodollars, Eurodollar credits could thus be increased freely on the basis of a relatively small fractional reserve held in New York. The risk was relatively small, since the banks which created the Eurodollars did not have to redeem them in either gold or foreign currencies. This was the concern of the U.S. Treasury and the foreign central banks, and the individual Eurobanks were always able to borrow from each other on a moment's notice. The danger of a general squeeze seemed extremely remote as far as the Eurobanks were concerned. By blocking the New York capital market to foreign borrowers, the Treasury and Federal Reserve in effect created a monster abroad which, for the time being at least, proved beyond either national or international control.

Compounding this problem were the huge liquid assets of the multinational corporations—estimated at more than $300 billion on the eve of the dollar crisis in January 1973. Once the corporate officials responsible for these funds became convinced that a second dollar devaluation was unavoidable, they rushed to hedge future commitments and to seek shelter for the endangered dollar balances. In the end, all the gadgets developed during the 1960s proved powerless in the face of the torrent of paper dollars.

INTERNAL "PROSPERITY" VERSUS INTERNATIONAL STABILITY

How was it possible that America, the most powerful and richest nation in the world, should experience such a rapid and far-reaching deterioration of its economic and political preeminence? Since Plato wrote his *Republic* in the fourth century before Christ, philosophers and political theorists have dreamed of the perfect state, which they would create through wise planning and by compelling those who disagreed to keep in step. Most of the social planners realized that they would have to confine their perfect society to their own limited nation-state, for the simple reason that they did not have the power to force the rest of the world into line. The solution was simple: cut off the "perfectly planned" nation-state from the rest of the world through control of exports and imports, restrictions on foreign travel, and creation of two types of money: a national currency which could be spent only within the border (inconvertible paper money in modern days); and international money, gold and silver, which would be held exclusively by the government and used only for purposes it deemed advisable. When President Roosevelt abandoned the gold standard in 1934, he explained that "the sound internal economic system of a nation is a greater factor in its well-being than the price of its currency in changing terms of the currencies of other nations . . . the United States seeks the kind of dollar which a generation hence will have the same purchasing power and debt-paying power as the dollar value we hope to attain in the near future."[12] Or, as Sir William Beveridge, the father of the full employment philosophy, put it a decade later: "Each country must work out its own full employment problem." In trying to isolate America from the "disturbing foreign influences," Roosevelt followed a well-trodden path. As did his predecessors and his epigoni of the 1960s and 1970s, he overlooked two important factors: that no man and no government is wise enough to plan the "perfect society" or the "perfect economy," or powerful enough to impose it upon the people except through totalitarian means; and that no nation, particularly a highly developed nation, exists in a vacuum.

The United States may be less dependent upon imports than Britain, the Netherlands, or Denmark, yet the American economy and the American way of life require the importation of large quantities of fuels, metals, and tropical products. In order to acquire these necessities, America must export goods, provide services, or draw on its foreign assets. It is a popular but misleading notion that America need not "let the tail," the $50 billion worth of international trade, "wag the dog," the more than $1.1 trillion American economy. America's international trade is not so much the "tail of the dog" as the water without which the dog can barely survive.

No politician is naive enough to suggest that the United States follow Plato's blueprint—or the Russian and the Chinese policies—and cut herself off from the rest of the world, but neither politicians nor the great mass of the people will admit that in order to be a part of the world, America must adjust to the world. In *The Wall Street Journal* (August 14, 1972), then Treasury Secretary George Shultz, for example, called for "the development of international rules of conduct." But these rules, he thought, "must leave room for that exercise of national sovereignty which all nations must retain regarding policies affecting the welfare of their citizens." We recognize "the growing economic interdependence among nations," but if we find it politically expedient to pursue an inflationary policy at home—for the welfare of the American people—we should be free to do so.

For centuries, governments have searched in vain for a way of combining the "needs for national sovereignty" with the "needs for international cooperation." Now the experts and politicians claim to have found the solution: floating exchange rates, which will supposedly enable the governments to assure ever rising prosperity within the country, without having to cut America off from the rest of the world. The dollar is to be permitted to "find its own level."

But what level? As long as consumption in the United States does not exceed production, and the world has confidence in the dollar, there is no need for a "floating" rate. The world will be happy to have a constant dollar as an international standard of value. But if consumption in America exceeds production, as it has since the 1950s, a "floating" dollar will prove to be just a euphemism for a progressively depreciating dollar. As long as the deficit spending continues, wages increase faster than productivity, consumption exceeds production, and savings are inadequate to maintain and expand the nation's productive capacity, the dollar will drift downward. And as the value of the dollar declines, the cost of essential imports will increase. In the end, America will be confronted with the same alternatives which face the nation today: to reduce consumption (because of the rising cost of imports), or to spend even less on the maintenance of the nation's productive capacity, which must lead to an ultimate collapse. It is not possible, for any length of time, whether exchange rates are fixed or floating, for the average unit cost in America to remain above world market levels, or for interest rates and profits to be maintained artificially below those of other money and capital markets.

A downward floating exchange rate means higher prices for imports, such as gasoline and coffee, and indirectly rising prices in general, which in turn must result in decreasing consumption and hence a lower standard of living, unless the government offsets the higher prices through the issuance of more paper money, which would further accelerate the inflation. The only way to stop the progressive decline of the purchasing power of the paper dollar, at home and abroad, is to limit consumption to the actual output of goods and services, with adequate reserves for depreciation and expansion. This policy is not an easy one to follow, since in an economy saturated with an inflationary mentality the emphasis tends to be upon consumption rather than savings.

According to the so-called Phillips curve, which Senator William Proxmire and many other experts regard as "one of the most rudimentary principles . . . in economic theory," a nation accepts a certain rate of chronic inflation in order to reduce unemployment to a socially acceptable level. Actually, this notion is far from "rudimentary" in the sense of being universally valid. It does not apply to situations of chronic inflation because it does not take into consideration the psychological effects of steadily decreasing monetary values, which make people rush into goods, whatever the price—gold, real estate, art objects, platinum, diamonds, anything which promises "security" or quick profits—while less and less capital is available for long-term investments and hence job opportunities.

SOFT MONEY VERSUS HARD MONEY

The nineteenth-century gold standard provided an international currency which created one large, closely interwoven international monetary and economic system, linking all major national economies. It functioned because for ninety-nine years, between Waterloo and the outbreak of World War I, the world experienced no major war or social unheaval. The nineteenth century was the age of the rising middle class, which, on the basis of past experience, felt that "we have gold, because we cannot trust governments." Under the gold standard, no government could pursue an inflationary policy because the volume of money and credit was limited by law to the available gold reserves. As prices rose and imports exceeded exports, gold had to be exported to pay for the import surplus, the gold reserves declined, and thus the supply of money and credit. A cost-push inflation was impossible because rising prices, and thus demand for credit, would promptly run into the ceiling set by the nation's gold reserves.

The ties between gold, the money supply, and prices were obviously not as rigid as economic models indicate.[13] World market as well as domestic prices fluctuated during the nineteenth century as the production of either goods or gold increased more rapidly, but the fluctuations were much smaller than those which the world has experienced since 1914. Above all, prices "fluctuated"; they did not increase continuously for decades on end.

The spirit of the nineteenth century did not survive World War I. The age of the middle class, which feared government domination, has given way to the age of the "common man," who expects the state to solve the problems he himself feels

unable to solve. For ideological and political reasons, the
twentieth century therefore rejects the automatic controls of
the gold standard because they hamper the freedom of governments to do what the governments think desirable or politically expedient. But in the end, entrusting the welfare of
the economy to the government involves a profound risk;
political expediency as a rule outweighs economic rationality
and necessity. This is exactly what happened in the United
States during the 1960s and 1970s.

REMOVING THE CONTROLS

Step for step, the American government has "unshackled"
itself from the restraints of the gold standard.[14] Under the New
Deal legislation of the early 1930s,[15] Americans were
prohibited from owning gold, thus making the dollar
nonconvertible within the United States. At the end of the war
in 1945, Congress, for no compelling reason, lowered the gold
reserves from 40 percent for Federal Reserve notes and 35
percent for member bank deposits to a flat 25 percent, thus
"freeing" more than $5 billion in gold reserves, which went a
long way to finance the postwar inflation well into the 1950s.[16]
Likewise without compelling reason, President Eisenhower,
as one of his last official acts, prohibited Americans by
executive fiat from owning gold abroad, thus depriving the
American public of a possible hedge against the progressive
cheapening of the dollar.

If Congress had not lowered the gold reserve requirements
in 1945, the country would have run out of "free gold" during
the Kennedy Administration. The great "prosperity" of the
early 1960s, financed through a vast expansion of credit, would
thus not have been possible. On the other hand, the country
might have been spared the grave economic and social dis-
locations of the late 1960s and 1970s, the end of which is not yet
in sight.

As the inflation continued, the government progressively

"unshackled" itself. In 1965, the 25 percent gold reserve requirements for member bank reserves—which constituted a restriction on the creation of bank credit—were removed,[17] "freeing another $5 billion of gold, which was enough to finance the inflation during the second half of the 1960s. In 1968 the reserve requirements behind the Federal Reserve notes were removed as well, thus eliminating the last restraint upon the government to inflate the currency further. At about the same time Congress voted to put the phrase "In God we trust" on the Federal Reserve notes.

After 1968 there was no more link between the paper dollar and gold as far as the domestic economy was concerned, thus making it possible for Washington to expand the supply of money and credit without restraints. Even so, the government maintained the fiction of international convertibility, although it warned that the gold window would be closed if foreign central banks were to try to convert their huge dollar holdings into gold. By the end of the 1960s, the headlong rush toward monetary chaos could have been stopped only through heroic efforts, for which the American people were not prepared, and which the government apparently did not even consider because of the dangerous political and social tensions throughout the country. The London gold pool was dissolved in March 1968 because it was no longer possible to maintain the value of the depreciating dollar at $35 per ounce of gold. A two-tier of gold prices was introduced:[18] a highly artificial official price of $35 which applied only to transactions between central banks and official monetary institutions; and the free market price which was expected to decline and stay below the official price, but which actually rose to more than $100 by 1973. In August 1971, President Nixon ended the international convertibility of the dollar;[19] in December 1971, under the pressure of the European creditor nations, America had to agree to increase the price of gold to $38; and in February 1973 the gold price was raised again to $42.22, the second devaluation of the dollar in fourteen months.

The introduction of floating exchange rates in 1973 removed another restraint upon inflation-minded governments in America and throughout the world. The floating of the dollar in relation to the six strong currencies of the European Common Market and to the Japanese yen was obviously advantageous for the central banks and economies of the hard money countries: it eliminated the necessity of maintaining a fixed dollar exchange rate by buying paper dollars of uncertain value, thus adding to the internal money supply. The picture is quite different from the American point of view. The official devaluation of a currency is a traumatic experience which calls for front-page headlines. A steadily downward floating exchange rate, on the other hand, lacks drama. As one Washington expert put it: "News about the dollar will henceforth disappear to the financial page." Politicians and bureaucrats will thus be able to continue their politically convenient policy of deficit spending and of providing the consumer with easy credit, without the public being made aware of the consequences through front-page headlines.

Unless there is a drastic change in the political philosophy of Congress, the Administration, and the bureaucracy, the floating of the dollar will constitute an invitation to more inflation.

NOTES

[1]Some Washington experts at times hinted that this might not be the case. For example, in his surprisingly frank address before the annual meeting of the International Monetary Fund in Tokyo in September 1964, Treasury Secretary Douglas Dillon, warned: "The risk is that a country might drift into heavy and continuous reliance upon such essentially short-term credit facilities (swap arrangements, IMF drawings, bilateral credit arrangements, etc.), delaying too long the necessary corrective action that should be taken to adjust its balance of payments."

[2]Not all economists agree that capital formation in the United States has been inadequate. (1) They point to the sharp rise in capital

investments during boom years, such as 1972/1973. But to the extent that these spurts of capital formation were financed through an expansion of credit rather than savings, the growth of capital investments, while adding to the supply of goods, also added to the inflationary demand. (2) There is obviously an optimum level for capital formation. Economists speak of the decreasing marginal productivity of capital. The United States may have reached this point in some areas, while Japan and Germany still have greater need for capital investments. (3) In a mature economy, such as the United States, an increasing share of the Gross National Product consists of services rather than goods, and capital investments per worker tend to be lower in most service industries. (4) While capital formation may be inadequate in some areas of the American economy, it could be excessive in others. While the railroads suffer from inadequate maintenance, the airlines may have overexpanded their facilities. The apparent inadequacy of capital formation in the United States may thus be due in part to the misallocation of the scarce capital resources. The end effect, as far as the economy and the value of the dollar is concerned, however, is the same, whether overall capital formation is inadequate or whether some of the savings are wasted.

[3]John Maynard Keynes, *The Economic Consequences of the Peace* (New York: Harcourt Brace & Howe, 1920), p. 20.

[4]The Consumer Price Index rose from 53.9 in 1945 to 125.3 in 1972 (1967=100).

[5]From $318.1 to $439.2 billion in 1954 dollars (Federal Reserve "Bulletin," March 1961, p. 362).

[6]From $127.5 to $200.3 billion (Federal Reserve "Bulletin," March 1951, p. 293, and March 1961, p. 318).

[7]From $20 to $56 billion (Federal Reserve "Bulletin," March 1951, p. 330, and March 1961, p. 344).

[8]1-4 Family Houses, from 45.2 to $141.8 billion (Federal Reserve "Bulletin," March 1961, p. 341).

[9]The deficit averaged $0.3 billion in 1947-1951; $1.4 billion in 1952-1956; and $3.5 billion in 1957-1960.

[10]To discourage the purchase of foreign securities and the sale of new foreign stock and bond issues in the New York market, a 15-22 percent Interest Equalization Tax was imposed in 1963. The purchase of foreign securities dropped by 50 percent within the next year, but foreign companies in turn began to borrow correspondingly

more heavily from American banks. In 1964 restraints were, therefore, placed on bank loans to foreign borrowers, and in 1968 the controls of direct American investments abroad were tightened.

[11]In 1960 only 8 American banks had foreign branches; in 1971, well over 50. The number of foreign branches rose from 124 to 577, with assets of $67 billion.

[12]From President Roosevelt's Message to the World Conference in London (*The New York Times*, July 4, 1933, p. 1).

[13]The best-known of these models is the one developed by David Hume around 1750, known as price-specie-flow.

[14]"As the President [Roosevelt] put it, they unshackled themselves and the federal government . . . They made the manipulation of the value of the currency an open and admitted instrument of public policy." John Morton Blum: *From the Morgenthau Diaries: Years of Crises 1928-1938*, (Boston: Houghton Mifflin, 1959), p. 75.

[15]The Emergency Banking Act of March 9, 1933; the Thomas Amendment of the Agricultural Adjustment of May 1933; and the Gold Reserve Act of January 1934.

[16]Between 1945 and 1955, the Consumer Price Index rose by almost 50 percent, from 76.9 to 114.5 (1947-1949=100).

[17]"It seems clear that conditions now call for some change in the U.S. gold cover requirements," declared Federal Reserve Chairman William McChesney Martin in January 1965. "If developments well within the range of possibility should be realized, the legal minimum could be penetrated soon, possibly within a year. Nevertheless, the dollar is strong, and so is the U.S. economy. Therefore, action on the gold cover legislation can be taken now, not to deal with a dollar crisis, but to maintain the dollar's current strength." The hearings before the congressional committee were limited to one day and the opposition was given no opportunity to testify, but while liberals called for a "clean sweep," the removal of all reserve requirements, President Johnson opposed the removal of the gold coverage behind the Federal Reserve notes, because of a "possible psychological effect." As *The Wall Street Journal* commented on January 29, 1965, "Retaining the 25 percent requirement [behind the Federal Reserve notes] would at least be a sign that the U.S. hasn't thrown overboard all restraints, all monetary discipline."

[18]Federal Reserve Board Chairman William McChesney Martin referred to the two-tier system as "a form of monetary gadgetry"

which will probably buy the country some time, but "the time has come to stop pussyfooting and get our accounts in order." (Speech before the Economics Club in Detroit, on March 18, 1969.)

[19]The suspension of dollar convertibility, according to Treasury Secretary George Shultz, "freed us to follow the domestic policies that we feel are the important ones, without having to worry so much about international developments." (*The Wall Street Journal*, August 14, 1972).

2

Gold vs. Fluctuating Fiat Exchange Rates

MURRAY N. ROTHBARD

Professor of Economics, Brooklyn Polytechnic Institute

Scarcely more than a year since it was signed, the Smithsonian Agreement, the "greatest monetary agreement in the history of the world" (in the words of President Nixon) lay in shambles. And so the world vibrates, with increasing intensity, between fixed and fluctuating exchange rates, with each system providing only a different set of ills. We apparently live in a world of perpetual international monetary crisis.

In this distressing situation, the last few years have seen the burgeoning of a school of economists who counsel a simple solution for the world's monetary illness. Since fixed exchange rates between currencies seem to bring only currency shortages and surpluses, black markets and exchange controls, and a chronic series of monetary crises, why not simply set all these currencies free to fluctuate with one another? This group of economists, headed by Professor Milton Friedman and the "Chicago School," claims to be speaking blunt truths in the name of the "free market." The simple and powerful case of the Friedmanites goes somewhat as follows:

Economic theory tells us the myriad evils that stem from any attempt at price controls of goods and services. Maximum price controls lead to artificially created shortages of the product; minimum controls lead to artificial unsold surpluses. There is a ready cure for these economic ills; they are caused not by processes deep within the free market economy, but by arbitrary government intervention into that market. Remove the controls, let the market processes have full sway, and the shortages and surpluses will disappear.

Similarly, the monetary crises of recent years are the product of government attempts to fix exchange rates between currencies. If the government of Ruritania fixes the "rur" at a rate higher than its free market price, then there will be a surplus of rurs looking for undervalued currencies, and a shortage of these harder currencies. The "dollar shortage" of the early postwar years was the result of the dollar being undervalued in terms of other currencies; the current surplus of dollars, as compared to West German marks or Japanese yen, is a reflection of the overvaluation of the dollar compared to these other currencies. Allow all of these currencies to fluctuate freely on the market, and the currencies will find their true levels, and the various currency shortages and surpluses will disappear. Furthermore, there will be no need to worry any longer about deficits in any country's "balance of payments." Under the pre-1971 system, when dollars were at least theoretically redeemable in gold, an excess of imports over exports led to a piling up of dollar claims and an increasingly threatening outflow of gold. Eliminate gold redeemability and allow the currencies to fluctuate freely, and the deficit will automatically correct itself as the dollar suppliers bid up the prices of marks and yen, thereby making American goods less expensive and German and Japanese goods more expensive in the world market.

Such is the Friedmanite case for the freely fluctuating exchange rate solution to the world monetary crisis. Any objection is met by a variant of the usual case for a free market. Thus, if critics assert that changing exchange rates introduce unwelcome uncertainty into world markets and thereby hinder international trade, particularly investment, the Friedmanites can reply that uncertainty is always a function of a free price system, and most economists support such a system. If the critics point to the evils of currency speculation, then Friedmanites can reply by demonstrating the important economic functions of speculation on the free commodity markets of the world. All this permits the Friedmanites to scoff at the timidity and conservatism of the world's bankers, journalists, and a dwindling handful of economists. Why not try freedom? These arguments, coupled with the obvious and increasingly evident evils of such fixed exchange rate systems as Bretton Woods (1945-1971) and the Smithsonian (1971-1973), are bringing an increasing number of economists into the Friedmanite camp.

The Friedmanite program cannot be fully countered in its details; it must be considered at the level of its deepest assumptions. Namely, are currencies really fit subjects for "markets"? Can there be a truly "free market" between pounds, dollars, francs, etc.?

Let us begin by considering this problem: suppose that someone comes along and says, "The existing relationship between pounds and ounces is completely arbitrary. The *government* has decreed that 16 ounces are equal to 1 pound. But this is arbitrary government intervention; let us have a free market between ounces and pounds, and let us see what relationship the market will establish between ounces and pounds. Perhaps we will find that the market will decided that 1 pound equals 14 or 17 ounces." Of course, everyone would find such a suggestion absurd. But *why* is it absurd? Not from arbitrary government edict, but because the pound is universally *defined* as consisting of 16 ounces. Standards of weight and measurement are established by common definition, and it is precisely their fixity that makes them indispensable to human life. Shifting relationships of pounds to ounces or feet to inches would make a mockery of any and all attempts to measure. But it is precisely the contention of the gold standard advocates that what we know as the *names* for different national currencies are not independent entities at all. They are not, in essence, different commodities like copper or wheat. They are, or they should be, simply names for different *weights* of gold or silver, and hence should have the same status as the fixed definitions for any set of weights and measures.

Let us bring our example a bit closer to the topic of money. Suppose that someone should come along and say, "The existing relationship between nickels and dimes is purely arbitrary. It is only the government that has decreed that two nickels equal one dime. Let us have a free market between nickels and dimes. Who knows? Maybe the market will decree that a dime is worth 7 cents or 11 cents. Let us try the market and see." Again, we would feel that such a suggestion would be scarcely less absurd. But again, why? What precisely is wrong with the idea? Again the point is that cents, nickels, and dimes are defined units of currency. The dollar is defined as equal to 10 dimes and 100 cents, and it would be chaotic and absurd to start calling for day-to-day changes in such definitions. Again, fixity of definition, fixity of units of weight and measure, is vital to any sort of accounting or calculation.

To put it another way: the idea of a *market* only makes sense between *different* entities, between different goods and services, between, say, copper and wheat, or movie admissions. But the idea of a market makes no sense whatever between different units of the *same* entity: between, say, ounces of copper and pounds of copper. Units of measure must, to serve any purpose, remain as a fixed yardstick of account and reckoning.

The basic gold standard criticism of the Friedmanite position is that the Chicagoites are advocating a free market between entities that are in essence, and should be once more, different units of the *same* entity, i.e., different weights of the commodity gold. For the implicit and vital assumption of the Friedmanites is that every national currency—pounds, dollars, marks, and the like—is and should be an independent entity, a commodity in its own right, and therefore should fluctuate freely with one another.

Let us consider: what *are* pounds, francs, dollars? Where do they come from? The Friedmanites take them at face value as things or entities issued at will by different central governments. The British government defines something as a "pound" and issues or controls the issue of whatever number of pounds it decides upon (or controls the supply of bank credit redeemable in these "pounds"). The United States government does the same for "dollars," the French government the same for "francs," and so on.

The first thing we can say, then, is that this is a very curious kind of "free market" that is being advocated here. For it is a free market in things, or entities, which are issued entirely by and are at the complete mercy of each respective government. Here is already a vital difference from other commodities and free markets championed by the Chicago School. Copper, steel, wheat, movies are all, in the Friedman *scheme*, issued by private firms and organizations, and subject to the supply and demand of private consumers and the free market. Only money, only these mysterious "dollars," "marks," etc., are to be totally under the control and dictation of every government. What sort of "free" market is this? To be *truly* analogous with free markets in other commodities, the supply of money would have to be produced only by private firms and persons in the market, and be subject only to the demand and supply forces of private consumers and producers. It should be clear that the governmental fiat currencies of the Friedmanite scheme cannot possibly be subject only to private and therefore to free market forces.

Is there any way by which the respective national moneys can be subject solely to private market forces? Is such a thing at all possible? Not only is the answer yes, but it is still true that the *origin* of all these currencies that the Friedmanites take at face value as independent entities, was, each and every one, as units of weight of gold in a truly private and free market for money.

To understand this truth, we must go back beyond the existing fiat names for money and see how they originated. In fact, we need go back only as far as the Western world before World War I. Even today, the "dollar" is not legally an independent fictive name; it is still legally defined by U.S. statute as a *unit of weight* of gold, now approximately one-forty-second of a gold ounce. Before 1914, the dollar was defined as approximately one-twentieth of a gold ounce. That's what a "dollar" *was*. Similarly the pound sterling was not an independent name; *it* was defined as a gold weight of slightly less than one-fourth of a gold ounce. Every other currency was also *defined* in terms of a weight of gold (or, in some cases, of silver.) To see how the system worked, we assume the following definitions for three of the numerous currencies:

1 dollar defined as one-twentieth of a gold ounce
1 pound sterling defined as one-fourth of a gold ounce
1 franc defined as one-hundredth of a gold ounce

In this case, the different national currencies are different in name only. In actual fact, they are simply different units of weight of the same commodity, gold. In terms of *each other*, then, the various currencies are immediately set in accordance with their respective gold weights, namely,

1 dollar is defined as equal to one-fifth of a pound sterling, and to 5 francs

1 franc is defined as equal to one-fifth of a dollar, and to
one-twenty-fifth of a pound
1 pound is defined as equal to 5 dollars, and to 25 francs.

We might say that the "exchange rates" between the various
countries were thereby fixed. But these were not so much
exchange rates as they were various units of weight of gold,
fixed ineluctably as soon as the respective definitions of weight
were established. To say that the governments "arbitrarily
fixed" the exchange rates of the various currencies is to say also
that governments "arbitrarily" define 1 pound weight as equal
to 16 ounces or 1 foot as equal to 12 inches, or "arbitrarily"
define the dollar as composed of 10 dimes and 100 cents. Like
all weights and measures, such definitions do not *have* to be
imposed by government. They could, at least in theory, have
been set by groups of scientists or by custom and commonly
accepted by the general public.

This "classical gold standard" had numerous and considerable economic and social advantages. In the first place,
the supply of money in the various countries was basically
determined, *not* by government dictates, but—like copper,
wheat, etc.—by the supply and demand forces of the free and
private market. Gold was and is a metal that has to be discovered, and then mined, by private firms. Its supply was
determined by market forces, by the demand for gold in
relation to the demand and supply of other commodities and
factors; by, for example, the relative cost and productivity of
factors of production in mining gold and in producing other
goods and services. At its base, the money supply of the world,
then, was determined by free market forces rather than by the
dictates of government. While it is true that governments were
able to interfere with the process by weakening the links
between the currency name and the weight of gold, the *base* of
the system was still private, and hence it was always possible to
return to a purely private and free monetary system. To the

extent that the various currency names were kept as strictly equivalent to weights of gold, to that extent the classical gold standard worked well and harmoniously and without severe inflation or booms and busts.

The international gold standard had other great advantages. It meant that the entire world was on a single money, that *money*, with all its enormous advantages, had fully replaced the chaotic world of barter, where it is impossible to engage in economic calculation or to figure out prices, profits, or losses. Only when the world was on a single money did it enjoy the full advantage of money over barter, with its attendant economic calculation and the corollary advantages of freedom of trade, investment, and movement between the various countries and regions of the civilized world. One of the main reasons for the great growth and prosperity of the United States, it is generally acknowledged, was that it consisted of a large free-trading area within the nation: we have always been free of tariffs and trading quotas between New York and Indiana, or California and Oregon. But not only that. We have also enjoyed the advantage of having one currency: one dollar area between all the regions of the country, East, West, North, and South. There have also been no currency devaluations or exchange controls between New York and Indiana.

But let us now contemplate instead what could happen were the Friedmanite scheme to be applied *within* the United States. After all, while a nation or country may be an important *political* unit, it is not really an economic unit. No nation could or should wish to be self-sufficient, cut off from the enormous advantages of international specialization and the division of labor. The Friedmanites would properly react in horror to the idea of high tariffs or quota walls between New York and New Jersey. But what of different currencies issued by every state? If, according to the Friedmanites, the ultimate in monetary desirability is for each nation to issue its own currency—for the Swiss to issue Swiss francs, the French their francs, and so on—then why not allow New York to issue its own "yorks," New Jersey its own "jersies," and then enjoy the benefits of a freely fluctuating "market" between these various currencies? But since we have *one* money, the dollar, within the United States, enjoying what the Friedmanites would call "fixed exchange rates" between each of the various states, we don't have any monetary crisis within the country, and we don't have to worry about the "balance of payments" between New York, New Jersey, and the other states.

Furthermore, it should be clear that what the Friedmanites take away with one hand, so to speak, they give back with the other. For while they are staunchly opposed to tariff barriers between geographical areas, their freely fluctuating fiat currencies could and undoubtedly would operate as crypto-tariff barriers between these areas. During the fiat money Greenback period in the United States after the Civil War, the Pennsylvania iron manufacturers, who had always been the leading advocates of a protective tariff to exclude more efficient and lower cost British iron, now realized that depreciating greenbacks functioned as a protective device: for a falling dollar makes imports more expensive and exports cheaper.[1] In the same way, during the international fiat money periods of the 1930s (and now from March 1973 on), the export interests of each country scrambled for currency devaluations, backed up by inefficient domestic firms trying to keep out foreign competitors. And similarly, a Friedmanite world *within* the United States would have the disastrous effect of functioning as competing and accelerating tariff barriers between the states.

And if independent currencies between each of the fifty states is a good thing, why not go still one better? Why not independent currencies to be issued by each county, city, town, block, building, person? Friedmanite monetary theorist Leland B. Yeager, who is willing to push thie *reductio ad absurdum* almost all the way by advocating separate moneys for each region or even locality, draws back finally at the idea of each individual or firm printing his own money. Why not? Because, Yeager concedes, "Beyond some admittedly indefinable point, the proliferation of separate currencies for ever smaller and more narrowly defined territories would begin to negate the very concept of money."[2] That it would surely do, but the point is that the breakdown of the concept of money begins to occur not at some "indefinable point" but *as soon as* any national fiat paper enters the scene to break up the world's money. For if Rothbard, Yeager, and Jones each printed his own "Rothbards," "Yeagers," and "Jones" and these were the only currencies, each among billions freely fluctuating on the market, it is clear that the world would be back in an enormously complex and chaotic form of barter and that all trade and investment would be reduced to a virtual standstill. There would in fact be no more *money*, for money *means* a general medium for all exchanges. As a result, there would be no money of account to perform the indispensable function of economic calculation in a money and price system. But the point is that while we can see this clearly in a world of "every man his own currency," the same disastrous principle, the same breakdown of the money function, is at work in a world of fluctuating fiat currencies such as the Friedmanites are wishing upon us. The way to return to the advantages of a world money is the opposite of the Friedmanite path: it is to return to a commodity which the entire world can and does use as a money, which means in practice the commodity gold.

One critic of fluctuating exchange rates, while himself a proponent of "regional currency areas," recognizes the classical argument for one world money. Thus, Professor Mundell writes:

It will be recalled that the older economists of the nineteenth century were internationalists and generally favored a world currency. Thus John Stuart Mill wrote *Principles of Political Economy*, vol. 2, p. 176:

... So much of barbarism, however, still remains in the transactions of most civilized nations, that almost all independent countries choose to assert their nationality by having, to their own inconvenience and that of their neighbors, a peculiar currency of their own.

Mill, like Bagehot and others, was concerned with the costs of valuation and money changing, not stabilization policy, and it is readily seen that these costs tend to increase with the number of currencies. Any given money *qua numéraire*, or unit of account, fulfills this function less adequately if the prices of foreign goods are expressed in terms of foreign currency and must then be translated into domestic currency prices. Similarly, money in its role of medium of exchange is less useful if there are many currencies; although the costs of currency conversion are always present, they loom exceptionally larger under inconvertibility or flexible exchange rates. Money is a convenience and this restricts the optimum number of currencies. In terms of this argument alone, the optimum currency area is the world, regardless of the number of regions of which it is composed.[3]

There is another reason for avoiding fiat paper currency issued by government and for returning instead to a commodity money produced on the private market (e.g., gold). For once a money is established, whatever supply of money exists does the full amount of "monetary work" needed in the economy. Other things being equal, an increase in the supply of steel, or copper, or TV sets is a net benefit to society: it increases the production of goods and services to the consumers. But an increase in the supply of money does no such thing. Since the usefulness of money comes from exchanging it rather than consuming it or using it up in production, an increased supply will simply lower its purchasing power; it will dilute the effectiveness of any one unit of money. An increase in the supply of dollars will merely reduce the purchasing power of each dollar, i.e., will cause what is now called "inflation." If money is a scarce market commodity, such as gold, increasing its supply is a costly process and therefore the world will not be subjected to sudden inflationary additions to its supply. But fiat paper money is virtually costless: it costs nothing for the government to turn on the printing press and to add rapidly to the money supply and hence to ruinous inflation. Give government, as the Friedmanites would do, the total and absolute power over the supply of fiat paper and of bank deposits—the supply of money—and we put into the hands of government a standing and mighty temptation to use this power and inflate money and prices.

I am not impressed when the Friedmanites become surprised and chagrined to see the government use its power to inflate in what they see as an excessive manner. It is virtually a law of politics that government will use the power that it is given. If it has the power to print money, it will use that power to the hilt—to pay for its own deficits, to subsidize favored businesses and groups in the society, and the like. Give to any group the compulsory monopoly over the money supply, and it will tend to use that power to the full: why should government be the exception? Certainly, the grisly inflationary record of government over the centuries should hold out no hope that government will suddenly become ascetic in its use of inflationary power.

Given the inherent tendency of government to inflate the money supply when it has the chance, the absence of a gold standard and "fixed exchange rates" also means the loss of balance-of-payments discipline, one of the few checks that governments have faced in their eternal propensity to inflate the money supply. In such a system, the outflow of gold abroad puts the monetary authorities on increased warning that they must stop inflating so as not to keep losing gold. Abandon a world money and adopt fluctuating fiat moneys, and the balance-of-payments limitation will be gone; governments will have only the depreciating of their currencies as a limit on their inflationary actions. But since export firms and inefficient domestic firms tend actually to favor depreciating currencies, this check is apt to be a flimsy one indeed.

Thus, in his critique of the concept of fluctuating exchange rates, Professor Heilperin writes:

> The real trouble with the advocates of indefinitely flexible exchange rates is that they fail to take into sufficient consideration the *causes of balance-of-payments disequilibrium*. Now these, unlike Pallas Athene from Zeus' head, never spring "full armed" from a particular economic situation. They have their causes, the most basic of which [are] internal inflations or major changes in world markets . . . "Fundamental disequilibria" as they are called . . . can-and-do happen. Often however, they can be avoided: if and when an incipient inflation is brought under control; if and when adjustments to external change are effectively and early made. Now nothing encourages the early adoption of internal correctives more than an outflow of reserves under conditions of fixed parities, always provided, of course, that the country's monetary authorities are "internationally minded" and do their best to keep external equilibrium by all internal means at their disposal. . . .[4]

Heilperin adds that the desire to pursue national monetary and fiscal policies without regard to the balance of payments is "one of the widespread and yet very fallacious aspirations of certain governments . . . and of altogether too many learned economists, aspirations to "do as one pleases' without suffering any adverse consequences." He concludes that the result of a fluctuating exchange rate system can only be "chaos," a chaos that "would lead inevitably . . . to a widespread readoption of exchange control, the worst conceivable form of monetary organization."[5]

If governments are likely to use any power to inflate fiat

currency that is placed in their hands, they are indeed almost as likely to use the power to impose exchange controls. It is politically naive in the extreme to place the supply of fiat money in the hands of government and then to hope and expect it to refrain from controlling exchange rates or going on to impose more detailed exchange controls. In particular, in the totally fiat economy that the world has been plunged into since March 1973, it is highly naive to expect European countries to sit forever on their accumulation of 80-odd billions of dollars—the fruits of decades of American balance-of-payments deficits—and expect them to allow an indefinite accumulation of such continually depreciating dollars. It is also naive to anticipate their accepting a continually falling dollar and yet do nothing to stem the flood of imports of American products or to spur their own exports. Even in the few short months since March 1973 central banks have intervened with "dirty" instead of "clean" floats to the exchange rates. When the dollar plunged rapidly downward in early July, its fall was only checked by rumors of increased "swap" arrangements by which the Federal Reserve would borrow "hard" foreign currencies with which to buy dollars.

But it should be clear that such expedients can only stem the tide for a short while. Ever since the early 1950s, the monetary policies of the United States and the West have been short-run expedients, designed to buy time, to delay the inevitable monetary crisis that is rooted in the inflationary regime of paper money and the abandonment of the classical gold standard. The difference now is that there is far less time to buy, and the distance between monetary crises grows ever shorter. All during the 1950s and 1960s the Establishment economists continued to assure us that the international regime established at Bretton Woods was permanent and impregnable, and that if the harder money countries of Europe didn't like American inflation and deficits there was nothing they could do about it. We were also assured by the same economists that the official gold price of $35 an ounce—a price which for long has absurdly undervalued gold in terms of the depreciating dollar—was graven in stone, destined to endure until the end of time. But on August 15, 1971, President Nixon, under pressure by European central banks to redeem dollars in gold, ended the Bretton Woods arrangement and the final, if tenuous, link of the dollar to redemption in gold.

We are also told, with even greater assurance (and this time by Friedmanite as well as by Keynesian economists) that when, in March 1968, the free market gold price was cut loose from official governmental purchases and sales, that gold would at last sink to its estimated nonmonetary price of approximately $10 an ounce. Both the Keynesians and the Friedmanites, equal deprecators of gold as money, had been maintaining that, despite appearances, it had been the *dollar* which had propped up *gold* in the free-gold markets of London and Zurich before 1968. And so when the "two-tier gold market" was established in March, with governments and their central banks pledging to keep gold at $35 an ounce, but having nothing further to do with outside purchases or sales of gold, these economists confidently predicted that gold would soon disappear as a monetary force to reckon with. And yet the reverse has happened. Not only did gold never sink below $35 an ounce on the free market, but the market's perceptive valuation of gold as compared to the shrinking and depreciating dollar has now hoisted the free market gold price to something like $125 an ounce. And even the hallowed $35 an ounce figure has been devalued twice in the official American accounts, so that now the dollar—still grossly overvalued—is pegged officially at $42.22 an ounce. Thus, the market has continued to give a thumping vote of confidence to gold, and has brought gold back into the monetary picture more strongly than ever.

Not only have the detractors of gold been caught napping by the market, but so have even its staunchest champions. Thus, even the French economist Jacques Rueff, for decades the most ardent advocate of the eminently sensible policy of going back to the gold standard at a higher gold price, even he, as late as October 1971 faltered and conceded that perhaps a doubling of the gold price to $70 might be too drastic to be viable. And yet now the market itself places gold at very nearly double *that* seemingly high price.[6]

Without gold, without an international money, the world is destined to stumble into one accelerated monetary crisis after another, and to veer back and forth between the ills and evils of fluctuating exchange rates and of fixed exchange rates without gold. Without gold as the basic money and means of payment, fixed exchange rates make even less sense than fluctuating rates. Yet a solution to the most glaring of the world's aggravated monetary ills lies near at hand, and nearer than ever now that the free-gold market points the way. That solution would be for the nations of the world to return to a classical gold standard, with the price fixed at something like the current free market level. With the dollar, say, at $125 an ounce, there would be far more gold to back up the dollar and all other national currencies. Exchange rates would again be fixed by the gold content of each currency. While this would scarcely solve all the monetary problems of the world—there would still be need for drastic reforms of banking and central bank inflation, for example—a giant step would have been taken toward monetary sanity. At least the world would have a *money* again, and the spectre of a calamitous return to barter would have ended. And that would be no small accomplishment.

NOTES

[1]On depreciating fiat currency as a protectionist device during the Greenback period, see Murray N. Rothbard, "Money, the State, and Modern Mercantilism," in H. Schoeck and J. W. Wiggins, eds., *Central Planning and Neomercantilism* (Princeton, N.J.: D. Van Nostrand, 1964), pp. 149-151.

[2]Leland B. Yeager, "Exchange Rates within a Common Market," *Social Research* (Winter 1958): 436-37. See also Yeager, "An Evaluation of Freely-Fluctuating Exchange Rates" (Ph. D. dissertation, Columbia University, 1952).

[3]Robert A. Mundell, *International Economics* (New York: Macmillan, 1968), p. 183.

[4]Michael A. Heilperin, *Aspects of the Pathology of Money* (London: Michael Joseph, 1968), p. 227.

[5]Ibid., pp. 222, 293.

[6]Jacques Rueff, *The Monetary Sin of the West* (New York: Macmillan, 1972), pp. 210-211.

3

No Shortage Of Gold

HANS F. SENNHOLZ

Professor of Economics,
Grove City College

Many economists seem to agree on the virtues of the gold standard. It limits the power of governments or banks to create excessive amounts of paper currency and bank deposits, that is, to cause inflation. It also affords an international standard with stable patterns of exchange rates that encourage international trade and investments. But the same economists usually reject it without much hesitation because of its assumed disadvantages. The gold standard, they say, does not allow sufficient flexibility in the supply of money. The quantity of newly mined gold is not closely related to the growing needs of the world economy. If it had not been for the use of paper money, a serious shortage of money would have developed and economic progress would have been impeded. The gold standard, they say, also makes it difficult for a single country to isolate its economy from depression or inflation in the rest of the world. It does not permit exchange rate changes and resists government controls over international trade and payments.

The gold standard does in fact make it difficult to isolate one country from another. After all, the common currency that is gold would invite exchanges of goods and services and thus thwart an isolationist policy. For this reason completely regimented economies cannot tolerate the gold standard that springs from economic freedom and inherently resists regimentation. The gold standard also exposes all countries that adhere to it to imported inflations and depressions. But as the chances of any gold inflation and depression that would follow such an inflation are extremely small, the danger of contagion is equally small. It is smaller by far than with the floating fiat standard that suffers frequent disruptions and uncertainties, or with the dollar-exchange standard that actually has inundated the world with inflation and credit expansion.

It must also be admitted that the gold standard is inconsistent with government controls over international trade and payment. But we should like to question the objection that the newly mined gold is not closely related to the growing needs of business and that a serious shortage of money would have developed without the issue of paper money. This popular objection to the gold standard is rooted in several ancient errors that persist in spite of the refutations by economists.

There is no shortage of gold today just as there has been no such shortage in the past. Indeed, it is inconceivable that the needs of business will ever require more gold than is presently available. Gold has been wealth and the medium of exchange in all of the great civilizations. Throughout history men have toiled for this enduring metal and have used it in economic exchanges. It has been estimated that most of the gold won from the earth during the last 10,000 years, perhaps from the beginning of man, can still be accounted for in man's vaults today, and in ornaments, jewelry, and other artifacts throughout the world. No other possession of man has been so jealously guarded as gold. And yet, we are to believe that today we are suffering from a serious shortage of gold and therefore must be content with fiat money.

Economic policies are the product of economic ideas. This is true also in the sphere of monetary policies and the organization of the monetary system. The advocates of government paper and the foes of gold are motivated by the age-old notion that the monetary system in scope and elasticity has to be tailored to the monetary needs of business. They believe that these needs exceed the available supply of gold which deprives it of any monetary usefulness and thus make it a relic of the distant past.

THE MONETARY NEEDS OF BUSINESS

With most contemporary economists the notion of the monetary requirements of business implies the need for an institution, organization, or authority that will determine and provide the requirements. It ultimately implies that the government must either establish such an institution or provide the required money itself. These writers accept, without further thought, government control over the people's money. Today, all but a few economists readily accept the apparent axiom that it is the function of the government to issue money and regulate its value. Like the great classical economists, they blindly trust in the monetary integrity and trustworthiness of government and the body politic. But while we can understand Hume, Thornton, and Ricardo, we are at a loss about the confidence of our contemporaries. We understand Ricardo when he proclaimed that "In a free society, with an enlightened legislature, the power of issuing paper money, under the requisite checks of convertibility at the will of the holder, might be safely lodged in the hands of commissioners. . . ."[1] The English economists had reason to be proud of their political and economic achievements and to be confident in the world's future in liberty. However, it is more difficult to understand the naive confidence of our contemporaries. After half a century of monetary depreciation and economic instability still to accept the dogma that it is the proper function of government to issue money and regulate its value reflects a high degree of insensibility to our monetary plight.

And yet, the world of contemporary American economics blindly accepts the dogma. True, we may witness heated debates between the Monetarists and Keynesians about the proper rate of currency expansion by government, or the proper monetary/fiscal mix of federal policy. But when their squabbles occasionally subside they all agree on "the disadvantages" of the gold standard and the desirability of fiat currency. They vehemently deny the only other alternative: monetary freedom and a genuine free market.

The money supply needs no regulation. It can be left to the free market in which individuals determine the demand for and supply of money. A person wants to keep a certain store of purchasing power, a margin of wealth in the form of money. It does not matter to him whether this wealth is represented by a few large units of money or by numerous smaller units with the same total purchasing power. He is not interested in an increase in the number of units if such an increase constitutes no addition to his wealth. This is not to deny that people frequently complain about their "lack of money" or their "need for more money." What they mean, of course, is additional wealth, not merely more monetary units with smaller purchasing power. This popular mode of expression probably has contributed to the spread of erroneous notions according to which monetary expansion is identical with additional wealth. Our present policies of inflation seem to draw public support from this primitive confusion.

More than 200 years ago John Law was a victim of this confusion when he stated that "a larger quantity (of money) employs more people than a smaller one. And a limited quantity can employ only a proportionate number." It also made Benjamin Franklin denounce the "want of money in a country" as "discouraging laboring and handicraft from coming to settle in it." And it made Alexander Hamilton advocate currency expansion for the development of the "vast tracts of waste land." But only additional real capital in the shape of plants and equipment can employ additional people at unchanged wage rates, or develop new tracts of land. Even without additional capital, a market economy readily adjusts to additions in the labor supply until every worker who seeks employment is fully employed. In this process of adjustment, however, wage rates must decline because of the declining marginal productivity of labor. Monetary expansion tends to hide this wage reduction as it tends to support nominal wages, or even may raise them, while real wages decline.

The "full employment" economists, such as Lord Keynes and his followers, recommend monetary expansion because of this very wage reduction. They correctly realize that institutional maladjustments may prevent a necessary readjustment and thus cause chronic unemployment. The labor unions may enforce wage rates that are higher than the market rates which inevitably leads to unemployment. Or political expedience may call for the enactment of minimum wage legislation that causes mass unemployment. Under such conditions the full employment economists recommend monetary expansion as a face-saving device for both the labor government and labor unions. While it alleviates the unemployment, it causes a new set of ominous effects. It originates the economic boom that will be followed by another recession. It benefits the debtors at the expense of the creditors. Finally, while it depreciates the currency, it causes maladjustment and capital consumption and destroys individual thrift and self-reliance. The effects of currency depreciation, no matter how expedient such a policy may be, are worse than the restrictive effects of labor legislation and union policies. Furthermore, monetary expansion as a face-saving device sooner or later must come to an end. If not soon abandoned by a courageous administration, it will destroy the currency. If it is abandoned in time, the maladjustments and restrictive effects of labor legislation and union policies will then be fully visible.

No matter how ominous and ultimately disastrous this array of consequences of currency expansion may be, it is immensely popular with the short-sighted and ignorant. After all, currency expansion at first generates an economic boom; it benefits the large class of debtors; it causes a sensation of ease and affluence; it is a face-saving device for popular but harmful labor policies; and last but not least, it affords government and its army of politicians and bureaucrats more revenue and power than they would enjoy without inflation. All these effects may explain the popularity of currency expansion, but they do not prove the necessity of expanding the stock of money for any objective reason. In fact, *an increase in the money supply confers no social benefits whatsoever.* It merely redistributes income and wealth, disrupts and misguides economic production, and as such constitutes a powerful weapon in a conflict society.

In a free market economy it is utterly irrelevant what the total stock of money should be. Any given quantity renders the full services and yields the maximum utility of a medium of exchange. No additional utility can be derived from additions to the money quantity. When the stock is relatively large, the purchasing power of the individual units of money will be relatively small. Conversely, when the stock is small, the purchasing power of the individual units will be relatively large. No wealth can be created and no economic growth can be achieved by changing the quantity of the medium of exchange. It is so obvious and yet so obscured by the specious reasoning of special interests spokesmen that the printing of another ton of paper money does not create new wealth. It merely wastes valuable paper resources and generates the redistributive effects mentioned above.

Money is only a medium of exchange. To add additional

media merely tends to reduce their exchange value, their purchasing power. Only the production of additional consumer goods and capital goods enhances the wealth and income of society. For this reason some economists consider the mining of gold a sheer waste of capital and labor. Man is burrowing the ground in search of gold, they say, merely to hide it again in a vault underground. And since gold is a very expensive medium of exchange why should it not be replaced with a cheaper medium, such as paper money?

If gold merely served as a medium of exchange, new mining would indeed be superfluous. But it is also a commodity that is used in countless different ways. Its mining therefore does enrich society in the form of ornaments, dental uses, industrial products, and the like. Gold mining is as useful as any other mining that serves to satisfy human wants.

THE LAW OF COSTS APPLIES TO MONEY

The great expense of gold mining and processing assures its limitation of quantity and therefore its value. Both gold and paper money are subject to the "law of costs" which explains why gold has remained so valuable over the millennia and why the value of paper money always falls to the level of costs of the paper. This law, which is so well established in economic literature, states that *in the long run the market price of freely reproducible goods tends to equal the costs of production*. For if the market price should rise considerably above cost, production of the good becomes profitable and in turn invites additional production. When more goods are produced and offered on the market, the price begins to fall in accordance with the law of demand and supply. Conversely, if the market price should fall below cost and inflict losses on manufacturers, production is restricted or abandoned. Thus, the supply in the market is decreased, which tends to raise the price again in conformity with the law of supply and demand. Of course, the law of costs does not conflict with the basic principle of value and price. Their determination originates in the consumers' subjective valuations of finished products.

The law of costs obviously is applicable to gold. When its exchange value rises, mining becomes more profitable, which will encourage the search for gold and invite mining of ore that heretofore was unprofitable because of low gold content or other high mining costs. When additional quantities of gold are offered on the market, its exchange value or purchasing power tends to decline in accordance with the law of supply and demand. Conversely, when its exchange value falls, the opposite effects tend to ensue.

That paper money is subject to the law of costs is vehemently denied by all who favor such money. After all, they retort, the profit motive does not apply to its production and management. Its exchange value may be kept far above its cost of manufacture through wise restraint and management by monetary authorities.

It must be admitted that the law of costs works slowly on money, more slowly indeed than on other goods. It may take several decades before the paper money exchange value falls to the level of manufacturing costs. After all, the fall is rather considerable, from the value of gold for which the paper money first substitutes to that of the printing paper. Few other commodities ever experience such a large discrepancy between market value and manufacturing costs when the law of costs begins to work. This original discrepancy does not refute the applicability of the law; it merely offers an explanation for the length of time needed for the price-cost adjustment.

It must also be admitted that a certain measure of restraint prevents an immediate fall of the paper money value to the level of manufacturing costs. Popular opposition prevents the monetary authorities from multiplying the quantity of paper issue too rapidly, which would depreciate its value at intolerable rates and lead to an early disintegration of the exchange economy. In a democratic society these monetary authorities and their political employers would soon be removed from office and be replaced by others promising more restraint.

But no matter who manages the fiat money the law of costs is working quietly and continuously. Certainly, the manufacturers do profit from a gradual expansion of the money supply. The profit motive is as applicable to money as it is to all the other goods. The only difference between the manufacturer of fiat money and that of other goods is the monopolistic position of the former and the normally competitive limitations of the latter. Who would contend that the incomes and fortunes of central bankers and the jobs of many thousands of their employees do not provide a powerful motive for currency expansion? To stabilize the stock of money is to deny them position and power and thus income and wealth.

The profit motive for fiat money expansion is even stronger with the administration in power and the thousands of politicians seeking the votes of their electorates. Election to high political office usually assures great personal fortune, prestige, and power, and successful politicians quickly rise from rags to riches. In order to be elected in a redistributive conflict society, commonly called the welfare society, the candidate for political office is tempted to promise his electorate any conceivable benefit. He may at first propose to tax the rich members of his society whose few votes may be ignored. When their incomes and fortunes no longer yield the additional revenue needed for costly handouts, called social benefits, the welfare politician resorts to deficit spending. That is to say, he calls for currency expansion that facilitates the government expenditures that hopefully win the vote and support of his electorate and thus assure his election. When seen in this light the profit motive is surely applicable to the manufacture of paper money.

Or, the politicians in power conduct full employment policies through easy money and credit expansion. In search of the popular boom that would assure their reelection, they spend and inflate and thus set into operation the law of costs. Who would believe that such policies are not motivated by the personal gains that accrue to the politicians in power?

This profit motive must be sharply distinguished from that in the competitive exchange economy. When encompassed by competition, the motive is a powerful driving force for the best possible service to the ultimate bosses, the consumers. It raises output and income, and leads to capital formation and high standards of living. In the case of the monopolistic manufacture of paper money by government authorities, the profit motive finds expression in currency expansion, which is inflation. In the end, when the law of costs has completely prevailed and the exchange value of money equals the cost of paper manufacture, not only the fiat money is destroyed but also the individual-enterprise private-property order. Inflation not only bears bitter economic fruits but also has evil social, political, and moral consequences.

NO OBJECTIVE FACTORS DETERMINE THE DEMAND FOR MONEY

The fundamental error that permeates the writings of most economists is the notion that the demand of money is a given quantity determined by objective factors. From John Law to John Maynard Keynes the idea emerged that the monetary requirements of business, as determined by these objective factors, demanded larger quantities of money than actually were available. In their analyses of the "requirements" one or several of the following factors invariably played a decisive role: the volume of trade, the average velocity of circulation, and the price level.

Such an approach is basically spurious and fruitless for an investigation of monetary phenomena because it is entirely holistic. That is, it makes social phenomena that merely are the result of individual motivation and action the starting point. Business and society, however, merely demand money inasmuch as the individual members demand money. Therefore, any investigation of monetary phenomena must begin with the motivations and actions of individuals.

When the holistic ambiguity is brushed aside, the money requirements of business consist of the cash which businessmen deem necessary for the proper operation of their businesses. Their cash demand is determined by their value judgments, not by any objective fact. And each one is motivated by his own concern, not by holistic considerations. Depending on his future plans and his anticipation of future needs, a businessman wants to maintain a certain cash balance. As the size and kind of his commodity inventory reflect his anticipation and planning, so does his cash holding reflect his deliberate demand for cash. Just as his inventory decisions tend to affect commodity prices—no matter how minute his influence may be—so also do his decisions regarding cash holdings affect the purchasing power of the money.

Admittedly, a person's demand for money depends on its purchasing power. At first glance, this explanation indeed moves in a vicious circle. It seems to explain the purchasing power of money by reference to the individual demand for money, and then the individual demand for money by reference to its purchasing power. In reality, though, the explanation is no less logical than that regarding the inventory. A businessman's inventory decisions are affected by present prices and by his anticipation of future prices. Yet, no economist will deny that it is this anticipation and the demand it creates that may affect inventory prices. The same is true with regard to money. Our knowledge of the recent purchasing power of money and our evaluation of future conditions induce us to keep a certain cash reserve. But our decisions undoubtedly affect the objective exchange value of the monetary unit. Although our knowledge and anticipation of a certain purchasing power help us to arrive at a certain demand for money, it is nevertheless our demand intensities that determine the purchasing power.

Before there was any monetary demand for precious metals, their value was determined solely by the industrial demand. When people began to use them as media of exchange, the monetary demand for the metals tended to enhance their market values. Of course, the people's demand decisions were affected by their knowledge of the metals' exchange values, which at that moment were determined solely by industrial demand. This regression analysis, which was first developed by Ludwig von Mises, endeavors to explain the first emergence of a monetary demand for a commodity that hitherto was used for industrial purposes only. It explains how the present purchasing power of money emerged as the result of both kinds of demand, monetary as well as industrial.

Changes in the purchasing power of money may be brought about by changes in the demand for money. If people decrease their money holdings, i.e., if their demand intensity for money declines, its purchasing power will decrease and prices of goods will rise. On the other hand, if people endeavor to increase their money holdings, its purchasing power will tend to increase, i.e., prices of commodities and services will tend to decline. Thornton, Ricardo, and especially the banking theorists made this observation in connection with their analyses of the trade cycles. But instead of making the individual, his motivation and action, the subject matter of their inquiries, they became entangled in holistic concepts such as "circulation" and its "rapidity" or "velocity." This unfortunate error led the banking theorists and their contemporary followers to place "rapidity of circulation" in the very center of their cyclical investigations. They were led to denounce "hoarding," which merely depicts a cash holding that is unusually great in the opinion of the observer, as being "deflationary" and thus detrimental to the economy. They were led to denounce speculation, the "overtrading of some bold projectors," as Adam Smith had called it, as the causative factor of an economic boom that ultimately had to lead to a bust. Up to this very day the notion of the average velocity of circulation has played a fateful role in monetary theory and policy.

Money is not merely in "circulation," it is always in the ownership of individuals, banks, business associations, governments, or other social organizations. Being always under the control of someone and in someone's cash holdings even when in transit, it is the object of individual valuation and employment. Some owners prefer larger cash reserves than others. Some are increasing theirs, others reducing theirs. If one individual increases his cash holding, which tends to increase the objective exchange value of the monetary unit, another may be reducing his, which fact will counteract the former tendency. Of course, in every cash transaction the buyer of a commodity reduces his cash holding while the seller increases his, which leaves the total cash holdings unchanged. Yet, this exchange may affect the purchasing power of the money. It reduces it if the exchange results from an increase in the intensity of the commodity demand or a decrease in the intensity of money demand. Other conditions being equal, the purchasing power of the monetary unit tends to decline and commodity prices to rise whenever the subjective value of the monetary unit declines or that of the commodity increases with either the buyer or seller or both.

The volume of trade and velocity analysis must always be spurious because it makes the national economy its object of investigation. In the realm of individual conduct there is no room for such concepts. As a potential buyer or seller the individual is guided by his subjective valuation of the economic good and that of the medium of exchange. His actions in turn exert an influence on the ratio of exchange that emerges on the market. How does a holistic equation in any way indicate this casual relation? While it aims at an analysis of the factors determining the value of money, it assumes commodity prices. In other words, in the very equation that is to explain the purchasing power of money these theorists assume an exchange ratio between commodities and money which in fact assumes a certain purchasing power of money. In the final analysis, the exchange equation is merely a mathematical game, with the economic proposition that the purchasing power of all the money spent in a given time equals the prices of the goods exchanged for the money.

ECONOMIC EXPANSION REQUIRES NO MONETARY EXPANSION

Changes in the dollar's purchasing power of money can also be brought about by changes in the supply of commodities and services, which in turn affect the demand for money in exchange. In this case we speak of "goods-induced" changes in purchasing power. If the supply of goods declines, other things being equal, the purchasing power of the medium of exchange necessarily declines. On the other hand, if the supply of goods increases while that of money remains unchanged, a tendency towards enhancement of the purchasing power of money results. This fact is probably the most popular reason advanced today for policies of monetary expansion. "Our expanding national economy," economic and monetary authorities proclaim, "requires an ever growing supply of money and credit in order to assure economic stability."

No one can seriously maintain that the present expansionary policies have brought about economic stability. During the last forty years of almost continuous monetary expansion the American economy underwent no fewer than six distinct depressions or recessions. It is obvious that the monetary expansion, whatever else it may have achieved, did not facilitate economic stability. Rather, it gave our age its economic characteristic—unprecedented instability.

Even if no other objection could be raised against the expansionary endeavors, the assumption of a constantly rising national product must be questioned. It is true that in terms of current dollars the national product probably will rise to astronomical figures, but in terms of real goods the national product can hardly be expected to rise much further in this era of extreme interventionism. Economic progress, if any, must be painfully slow. The economy is carrying a tax burden larger than any in history. Excessive taxes by all levels of government, federal, state, district, and local, are destroying the revenue sources they tax and are inflicting penalties on progress. They have quelled individual incentive and are consuming productive capital. They are rising steadily and taking more than $350 billion a year, which amounts to more than one-quarter of the value of everything produced in the nation. Inflation even accelerates the destruction through taxation inasmuch as it increases money income and prices, and thus subjects the citizens to higher and higher rates of taxation.

Our skepticism as to future growth of the national product is strengthened by the present disintegration of the world division of labor. Nationalization of vital industries built with European capital has become a popular policy in most underdeveloped areas of the "free world." The Far East, Middle East, North Africa, South Africa, and some parts of South and Central America are in a political turmoil. Trade relations are deteriorating to the detriment of all nations participating in the world division of labor. The United States is also affected by the disintegration of the world market. For these and other reasons stemming from the sway of radical collectivism in most parts of the world and the disintegration of the world monetary order, we cannot share the popular belief in a continuously rising national product.

But even if it should rise, there is no need for credit expansion. On the contrary, a rising national product presupposes absence of monetary adventures that lead to capital consumption and malinvestment. Rising productivity without monetary expansion would result in lower product prices and higher wages. Throughout most of the nineteenth century prices were declining because of capital accumulation and higher labor productivity. For the same reason wages were rising. However, declining prices, according to prevailing monetary opin-

ion, call for more money until a desirable "price level" has
been attained. The "monetary requirements of business," as
seen by some economists, are conditioned by the "level" of
commodity prices. A falling level is assumed to indicate the
need for more money; a stable level indicates the desirable
state of stability; and a rising level reveals an excess of money
over the true requirements. The level itself is said to vary
directly with the quantity of money in circulation. That is, it
rises or falls in proportion to the increase or decrease of the
money supply.

The notion of a price "level" must be rejected for being
deficient and misleading. Changes in the quantity of money do
not affect the prices of all goods at the same time and to the
same degree. They cause price upheavals, not uniform
changes of all prices. Just as the prices of all commodities and
services are determined by their demand and supply, so is the
purchasing power of money. If the supply increases, the
holders of the new money—either the federal government or
other institutions and individuals—are in the position to buy
more goods than they did before. Now, the prices of those
goods that are demanded in additional quantities tend to rise
while those of other goods at first remain unaffected. The
sellers of the products whose prices are rising reap an additional income. They, too, can now purchase more than they could
before the increase of the money supply. Thus, prices continue
to rise until all prices have risen, but they do not increase
simultaneously and to the same degree. This fact causes some
people to gain and some people to lose. The sellers of products
or services marketed at higher prices obviously must gain if
they can continue to buy in markets not yet affected by price
rises. On the other hand, the sellers of products whose prices
have not yet risen must lose if they are purchasers in markets
with higher prices. When the readjustment process finally
comes to an end, the material position of all people has been
affected.

The old quantity theory failed to recognize these changes in the price structure and in the material position of the holders of money. It asserted a constant relationship between the money supply and "the level of prices." But there are neither proportional changes of commodity prices nor a constant relation between the volume of money and prices.

Even if we were to admit the existence of price "levels," we still would have to question the need for more money whenever prices are falling. In a market economy unhampered by monetary experiments, prices would decline continuously and wages would rise. The purchasing power of the monetary unit would increase as a result of rising productivity and output. Of course, individual prices may nevertheless increase due to changes in consumer preferences and production conditions.

The advocates of price stability dread price declines. Only if price declines are avoided, they believe, can business operate profitably. Undeniably, however, the profitability of business arises from the spread between the prices of products and the business costs, not from price stability. It is very conceivable that business is profitable while prices decline, provided costs decline equally or to an even greater degree. During the last three decades of the nineteenth century prices declined steadily, and yet it was a period of unprecedented capital accumulation and economic growth. Although hourly wages rose continuously, business costs declined because of rapidly rising productivity.

An economist who advocates monetary expansion for the sake of price stability faces the following problem: who is to get this additional money? Is it to go to the government for additional spending? Such a proposal would surely find a willing ear with politicians and civil servants. But then the question arises: who are to be the beneficiaries of this government spending? No matter what the answer, the government spending will be a point of contention with the various pressure groups struggling with each other for the spoils of the additional spending.

Or business may get the additional money. The central bank may buy securities in the open market and thus increase bank reserves. Now, should it buy commercial bills, bankers' acceptances, U.S. Treasury bills, certificates, or notes and bonds? Whatever it should decide upon, the purchase will benefit some people and discriminate against others. Again, a general struggle would arise among the various groups of potential beneficiaries. Finally, there are two more methods of increasing the money supply: the central bank may lower the reserve requirements of member banks, or it may lower the bank rate, or discount rate, in order to facilitate the expansion. Again, arbitrary decisions have to be made. How much of the additional money should go to the various banks in various parts of the country, how much to country banks or city banks? Also, if the discount rate is to be lowered, the capital market, too, deserves extra consideration. All these problems indicate irrefutably that an increase of the money supply involves many arbitrary authoritative decisions.

As has already been demonstrated above, whoever gets the money first will benefit from it. Let us assume it is poured into the building industry, which is a favorite child of the interventionist state. Then there will be more building activity than there otherwise would be. The building industry will prosper and attract, through the operation of higher prices, additional labor and capital from other industries. A building boom will develop. It will come to an end as soon as the industry has adjusted to the money influx. The building industry will suffer from acute unemployment if, in the next year, the monetary authorities should decide to pour the money into different industries. The building industry thus depends on continuous government help in the form of inflationary injections. It becomes a highly unstable industry subject to the mercy of the monetary authorities. While it becomes so dependent on additional money, it will form a militant pressure group to assure an adequate share of the new money. Other industries will form similar pressure groups eager to attain their proper shares. Ultimately, the annual increase of the money supply will have to be raised continuously. In other words, there is no stopping point once the authorities embark upon a policy of monetary expansion in order to assure price stability.

Wherever the money first enters the economy, it depresses the interest rate below that of the market. This effect is inevitable, for the additional money would find no borrowers at the unhampered market rate. But as soon as the interest rate is lower than the unhampered rate, economic maladjustment takes place. At the lower interest rate some businessmen will be eager to borrow additional funds and embark upon additional purchases. They will withdraw capital and labor from other employments and employ less efficient labor than was hitherto unemployed. Wages and other factor prices will rise until more and more businesses become unprofitable. A recession will finally set in. In other words, an increase of the money supply sets into motion the effects described by the trade cycle theory. This is true not only with an increase of 10 percent, but also of 5 percent of even 1 percent. Of course, the effects of a 1-percent increase will be milder than one of 10 percent.

A policy of monetary expansion thus presents us with the insoluble problem of distributing the additional money supply. It depends on authoritative discretion. It opens the gates of corruption and pressure politics. It makes the recipients dependent on continuous government help. And it causes the booms followed by recessions. It must be rejected without hesitation.

Despite these problems, monetary expansion continues at ever accelerating rates. The political pressures for economic redistribution generate larger and larger fiscal deficits that make currency expansion politically expedient and unavoidable. This is why the gold standard that makes the quantity of money independent of government is totally unacceptable to a society committed to redistributive policies. Such a society prefers to listen to a host of opportunist economists who applaud the popular policies and decry the gold standard. Their assertion of the shortage of gold must be seen in this light.

NOTE

[1]David Ricardo, "Principles of Political Economy and Taxation," in Piero Sraffa, ed., *The Works and Correspondence of David Ricardo* (Cambridge, England: University Press for the Royal Economic Society, 1951), I, 362.

4

To Restore World Monetary Order

HENRY HAZLITT, Author

Wilton, Connecticut

As we talk here tonight the world is in a monetary crisis. Within the last six weeks the American dollar, considered for the last thirty years as the very linchpin or anchor of the free world monetary system, has been devalued. Some currencies have been devalued along with it; some have been upvalued; most have been allowed to "float." In recent weeks the world's leading foreign exchange markets have even been officially closed.

Nobody seems quite sure what any currency will be worth tomorrow. For the last forty years we in the United States have had no assurance regarding how much goods and services our dollar would buy the following year. We only knew that it would buy less, but we could never tell exactly how much less. Now we do not even know what any currency will buy next year in terms of any other currency.

There is a temptation to say: "What's the point in discussing the subject now? Let's wait till the dust settles." But it may be a long time before the dust settles. It hasn't really settled for the last fifty-nine years. And it may very well be—I personally think it is—precisely when the turmoil and uncertainty are at their height, that it is the function and duty of those of us who professionally study these questions to try to bring whatever clarification we can to these grave problems, and to urge the reforms necessary to restore monetary stability, integrity, and order.

We can only understand the problems if we get back to fundamentals and the long historic view. Our present national and world monetary crisis is not the result simply of the mistakes that President Nixon and his advisers may have made since he came into office. *In its monetary policies the world has been on a disaster course for at least the last half century.* The trouble began with the wartime inflation that broke out shortly after 1914 in practically all of the world's developed countries. At the end of that war the victors, vanquished, and neutrals alike, found themselves with immensely expanded currency and credit. They mistakenly diagnosed their predicament as a "shortage of gold."

There was indeed a shortage of gold in relation to the immensely expanded volume of fiduciary media ostensibly convertible into gold. So at conferences in Brussels in 1921 and at Genoa in 1922 the principal industrial nations agreed to "economize" gold by adopting what was called a gold exchange standard. This probably should have been called a dollar and sterling standard, and later simply a dollar standard. It meant that the central banks of other nations could count their holdings of U.S. dollars as part of their "reserves." This meant, in other words, that they could count their paper dollars as added reserves against which they could in turn issue more paper francs, guilders, lire, or whatnot. Of course, this encouraged and almost forced a further world inflation.

The detailed way in which the gold exchange or dollar

standard worked to insure continuous world inflation has been best explained by M. Jacques Rueff, the eminent French economist, in innumerable articles and several important books over the last five decades, of which I would especially like to mention *The Balance of Payments*, published in 1967 (New York: Macmillan). M. Rueff has explained how the gold exchange standard systematically brings about a chronic balance-of-payments deficit in a reserve currency country because that country is under no pressure to correct the deficit. The gold exchange standard systematically brings about a growing world inflation because the debtor country, if it is a reserve currency country, does not lose, when it "pays" its debts, what its creditor countries gain.

So much for the period from 1922 to 1944. In the latter year, the representatives of forty-three nations, chiefly under the guidance of Lord Keynes of England and Harry Dexter White of the United States, agreed at Bretton Woods on a scheme calculated to cause a far greater expansion of paper money inflation. The Bretton Woods plan embodied the gold exchange standard, but it carried the principle even further. Each country was asked to fix an official "par value" for its currency. It was under no obligation to maintain that par value by making its currency convertible into gold at that rate. However, it was under an obligation to maintain its currency unit within 1 percent of that value by buying or selling other currencies, principally dollars, when its own currency showed signs of departing from that value.

Only one country, the United States, was under obligation to maintain its currency within 1 percent of its par value, fixed in gold at $35 an ounce, by agreeing to buy and sell gold on demand at that rate. It was not obliged to do this on the demand of any private person anywhere who presented dollars, but only on demand of a foreign central bank. This was still another device for "economizing" gold.

It is important to note that what was wrong with this system was not primarily technical. If all other countries had refrained

from inflation and had bought and sold dollars when required
to retain their own currency at a fixed parity, and if above all
the U.S. government had refrained from inflation and bought
dollars from and sold gold to foreign central banks on demand,
the system could have worked smoothly enough. All other
currencies would have maintained their fixed rate to the dollar,
the dollar would have maintained its fixed rate to gold, and so
all currencies would have maintained a fixed rate to gold.

To repeat: the trouble was not primarily technical. What was
wrong was that no direct discipline was put on any country but
the United States to keep its currency always convertible into
gold. The American authorities did not seem to have the
slightest realization of the immense responsibility that had
been put upon them to uphold the whole world monetary
network by refraining rigorously from inflation in order to
maintain continuous gold convertibility.

But it was in order to permit and encourage inflation (though
no one dared to state it so bluntly) that the whole Bretton
Woods structure had been set up. It did permit an enormous
world inflation, although it did not, as the years went on,
permit *enough* inflation to satisfy the government officials of
most of the member countries, including our own.

And so successive steps were taken to validate or consolidate
past national inflations and to make bigger future inflations
possible. There was not a single participating currency that was
not devalued at least once, and some were devalued many
times. The British pound, whose par value up to 1931 had been
$4.86, was devalued in September 1949 from $4.03 to $2.80.
That action touched off twenty-five devaluations of other
currencies within a single week. Then in November 1967 the
pound was devalued again from $2.80 to $2.40. The French
franc and other leading currencies were devalued many times.

(Let me add here as a personal note, that I was repeatedly
unable to obtain from the International Monetary fund, when
writing my weekly economic column for *Newsweek*, any complete record or tabulation of the number of devaluations of

their currencies by members of the Fund. So far as I know, the huge statistical department of the IMF has failed to put together such a simple one-page or single-figure tabulation to the present day.)

After about 1957, the dollar itself began to get into chronic trouble as a result of our own inflation. Our Presidents and monetary managers attempted to solve these problems by a succession of hastily improvised expedients to get by each emergency. In 1945, the percentage of gold reserves required against Federal Reserve notes was reduced from 40 percent to 25. In 1965 the gold backing required for Federal Reserve deposits was eliminated. In 1967 the requirement for any gold cover even for outstanding Federal Reserve notes was removed. In 1968, a two-tier gold system was adopted.

Desperate expedients were adopted in still other directions. Beginning in July 1963, under the false belief that our balance-of-payments deficit was caused by our investments abroad, a penalty tax was placed on purchases of foreign securities. This tax was extended in later years, together with other restrictions on foreign investments. These restrictions still exist.

All these expedients failed, of course, because our government continued to run up huge deficits in the federal budget, and to permit or create huge increases in the supply of paper money and credit. The governments of the world blamed everything but their own inflationary policies. Once more it was urged, as at Genoa in 1922 and at Bretton Woods in 1944, that the real trouble was not prior inflation but a "shortage of gold."

So the Special Drawing Rights were invented. This was thought a brilliant stroke. Instead of each country printing its own paper money, and so depreciating not only the purchasing power of each unit of that money in terms of goods, but also in terms of other currencies, why not have all the countries collectively issue a new unit of paper money, permit this new money, these "SDRs," to be used as reserves against which each country could issue more of its own paper money, call this new money "paper gold," and get each country to agree to accept up to a given amount of it, instead of gold, in settlement from other countries?

And so 3.4 billion units of these SDRs were allocated on January 1, 1970, another 3.0 billion units on January 1, 1971, and a third 3.0 billion units on January 1, 1972, making a total of some 9.4 billion SDRs, each ostensibly equal to the value of a dollar when the dollar was $35 an ounce. Even this huge amount, created out of thin air by international fiat, was not "enough."

The United States openly suspended gold payments on August 15, 1971. Within fourteen months the dollar was devalued twice—first by 8.57 percent on December 18, 1971, and then by 10 percent on February 12, 1973.

Yet today practically all the new "solutions" to the latest crisis are proposals to make it possible to print still more paper money for still more inflation to save us from the consequences of previous inflation.

It would be impossible to analyze all of these schemes here. To save time and effort I shall disregard all private or individual proposals and concentrate on the set of proposals, elaborated at an overall length of nearly thirty pages, in the annual report of the President's Council of Economic Advisers on January 31, 1973. These we may take to be the official proposals of the U.S. government.

It would be hard to imagine a more ominous scheme. It is put forward for the most part in technical euphemisms that obscure realities, but what it amounts to is this:

There is to be, of course, "increased flexibility of exchange rates." The guide to what should be done by any one nation (or central bank) is the amount of "reserves" that it holds. "Disproportionate changes in reserves in either direction [are] to be used as the primary indicator of the need for balance-of-payment adjustment." In plainer English, if the reserves of one nation got "too low," it would be obliged to devalue its currency unit; if its reserves got "too high," it would be obliged to revalue its currency unit upward. In other words, it would be encouraged to continue to follow rash inflationary policies because the penalties would be removed: it need not pay its debts 100 percent on the dollar in which they were contracted, but periodically could tell its foreign and domestic creditors that its IOUs would be paid off at only 90 percent or less of their original value.

On the other hand, a country would be penalized for following prudent monetary and fiscal policies and refraining from inflation. For in that case it would almost certainly gain reserves from the inflating countries. Therefore it would be obliged to upvalue its currency unit, that is, to bring about deflation and lower prices at home, and so to hurt its export trade by initially making its export prices higher for the nationals of other countries.

This is what the Council of Economic Advisers calls making "discipline symmetrical for both deficit and surplus countries." That is, you make discipline "symmetrical" not only by rewarding the heedless countries for inflating by allowing them and even requiring them to keep devaluing, but you "symmetrically" punish the prudent countries for not inflating by requiring them to upvalue.

This part of the Economic Advisers' plan implies fixed or "established" official exchange rates, subject, however, to constant change. But the Advisers also tell us that if other countries wished, "the U.S. proposal would permit either transitional or indefinite periods of floating." Apparently, anything is to be tolerated except a currency that keeps its value.

We come now to the most ominous part of the U.S. plan. The international monetary system must have what the Advisers call "adequate reserves." As they explain: "Failure to provide the system with adequate reserves puts deflationary pressure on deficit countries." Translating this into plainer English, unless we keep supplying the more recklessly inflat-

ing countries with "adequate reserves," we are in danger of
discouraging them from inflating further. This must at all costs
not be allowed to happen.

Of what are these reserves to be composed? Let me quote:
"The U.S. proposal envisages an increase in the importance of
the SDR . . . [and] a gradual diminution of the role played by
gold in the international monetary system" [pp. 123-24].
"From the end of 1969 to the end of October, 1972, gross
international official reserves increased from $78 billion to
$152 billion, or almost 100 percent in 3 years" [p. 128]. The
implication seems to be that this was not enough.

In any case, "For the future the United States supports
movement toward increasing reliance on the SDR as the
primary source of world reserve growth and toward progressive reduction in the role of gold as a reserve asset. The
U.S. proposal also assumes that currencies [i.e., U.S. dollars]
will also play a much smaller role in reserve holdings in the
future than they do today." The SDRs are to be "the primary
international reserve asset. They should become the formal
unit of account of the system, to serve as the common
reference point for currency rates and as a common measure of
the value of reserve assets" [p. 129].

"The rules of the International Monetary Fund should also
be changed to permit SDRs to be used in all IMF transactions
now permitting or requiring gold. SDRs would thus truly
become the basic international money. . . . The United States
believes that the role of gold in the international monetary
system should continue to diminish, and would support order-
ly procedures to facilitate that process" [p. 130].

So there you have it. The U.S. government wants to reduce
the value of its own currency unit by reducing the world
demand for it. It still has the largest gold holdings in the world
(some $11 billion at the last method of counting), but it wants to
be sure that these are devalued to the maximum extent by
being permanently demonetized.

And then in place of all this it wants to give the international bureaucrats the unlimited power by their mere fiat to create out of thin air the basic money we are all to be obliged to use and trust. Paper money issued by an international institution, the IMF, is to be allocated periodically by an arbitrary political formula to the various nations or their central banks. This paper is to serve as "reserves" for whatever paper money the individual nations choose to print. These paper SDRs are to serve as "reserves" simply because the individual central banks have agreed in advance so to accept them. It will not be necessary for any central bank to hold anything real. There is no provision for these SDRs to be redeemed in anything real. In fact, no government, no bank, and no individual has any legal obligation to redeem even a pro rata amount of SDRs. There is no obligor. As the former central banker, John Exter, has put it, an SDR is not even an IOU, but a Who Owes You.

At best the SDRs are an attempt to substitute international debts for gold. What they do is to entitle some countries to be automatic borrowers by obliging others to be automatic lenders.

It is obvious that the proposal of the Economic Advisers is merely a formula for a perpetual and unlimited world inflation. It will be in some respects worse than individual national inflation because it will not be as visible. When Ruritania inflates faster than other countries, this soon becomes manifest either by a depreciation of its currency unit in terms of other countries' currency units, or by a depletion of its reserves. But this world inflation through paper SDRs will only be revealed through a continued rise in world prices. As the more reckless-ly inflating countries will be continuously running short of even their SDR reserves, and the more prudently managed countries will be continually obliged to accept them, the more prudent will continually be subsidizing and paying for the inflations of the reckless countries.

If this plan were to be adopted, the IMF bureaucracy could apparently bypass even Congress or any other national assembly in providing more inflation.

For the very reason that it puts such unrestricted power into the hands of the world's central bank bureaucracy, there is a frightening likelihood that some such plan will be adopted. The only worse scheme I know of is the *New York Times'* editorial proposal of February 20, 1973, that "The world now needs a central bank to provide *unlimited* [italics mine] support for any nation whose currency is in trouble." Here is the most enticing invitation to reckless national inflation that could be imagined. But perhaps this is really no different from the Economic Advisers' proposal, with the IMF standing for that central bank and handing out SDRs in exchange for no value received whatever.

Of course, what the world really needs is the exact opposite of all this. A nation or central bank that has got itself into trouble through its own imprudence should be obliged to borrow in the open market and at whatever rate its credit standing warrants. It was a mistake of the International Monetary Fund from the beginning to grant any country automatic credit. Instead of issuing still more SDRs through the IMF, the SDRs already allotted should be retired. What each nation originally got is a matter of record; it should be asked to turn back that amount. The nations that have passed some of them on should be allowed to buy them back from present holders at the existing market rate for their own currencies. Then the IMF itself should be dismantled, and asked to return its own gold holdings to its member countries in proportion to the respective quotas paid in. The IMF has served merely as a world inflation factory. It imposes a constant threat of more inflation as long as it exists.

These are, of course, only the first steps in reform. Eventually, what we need is not to phase out what remains of the gold standard, as the Economic Advisers suggest, but to return to a full gold standard.

The reason for this proposal is clear and imperative. The constant convertibility of a currency into gold on demand, and to any amount, and to anybody who holds it, is necessary because experience has shown this to be the only way to prevent unlimited paper money inflation. David Ricardo stated the principle succinctly in 1817:

> Though it [paper money] has no intrinsic value, yet, by limiting its quantity, its value in exchange is as great as an equal denomination of coins, or of bullion in that coin. . . . Experience, however, shows that neither a State nor a Bank ever have had the unrestricted power of issuing paper money without abusing that power; in all States, therefore, the issue of paper money ought to be under some check and control; and none seems so proper for that purpose as that of subjecting the issuers of paper money to the obligation of paying their notes either in gold coins or bullion.

In other words, it is not for some purely "technical" reason that we need convertibility into gold on demand, but because we cannot otherwise trust the issuers, whether banks or politicians, to limit the supply.

It is not gold that carries some irrational mystique, but paper money. The mystique is the naive assumption that we can trust politicians or bureaucrats to issue paper money without their grossly abusing the power to do so.

It is not enough for those of us who believe in the restoration of the gold standard merely to ask for this—period. We have to recognize the tremendous obstacles, both political and economic, in the way of returning to that standard. And we have to answer four main questions:

1. What are the immediate steps to be taken?
2. What interim policies should be followed?
3. How can we solve the tremendously difficult problem of fixing a rate, which will be neither inflationary nor deflationary, at which convertibility can be announced and maintained?
4. What kind of gold standard should be set up?

The first question can be answered mainly by spelling out what we should *stop* doing:

1. A first step would be for our Federal Reserve authorities to stop printing more paper money and credit, to stop pumping funds into the money market. That is precisely what has gone into the process of inflation.

2. In order to remove any excuse, the federal government should start to balance its budget at the earliest possible moment, and entirely by slashing its grossly swollen expenditures, not by imposing still heavier taxes.

3. The Federal Reserve authorities should abandon all efforts to hold down short-term interest rates, either by pumping more funds into the money market, or by fixing an unjustifiably low discount rate, or by threats against individual banks for allegedly charging excessive interest. Rates should be left to competition in the free market.

4. The U.S. government should immediately repeal the laws which forbid or restrict private Americans from owning, buying, selling, and making contracts in gold.

The removal of this latter prohibition would have an instantaneous effect which it would be difficult to overestimate. It would not only remove an inexcusable abridgment of human liberty, but would go far to restore clarity to our monetary thinking. A really open gold market would appear within a few days. This would reflect the true discount on the dollar and on every other paper currency. A weight of gold, an ounce or a gram, would provide a common objective standard in terms of which the market value of all the world's currencies would be quoted.

Gold would immediately become, whether monetized anywhere or not, a de facto world currency in terms of which international transactions would once more be made. Exporters and other creditors would want to be paid in money or in a commodity of dependable long-term value. This does not necessarily mean that actual gold would change hands in each transaction, but that gold would be a money of account, a numéraire, in terms of which payment would be specified.

So much for the steps to monetary reform that could be taken, or at least announced, within a week, if the will existed to take them.

We come now to the question of what interim policies should be followed. We might call this Phase Two. The first step, I think, would be to try to arrange with our creditors some way of funding our huge overhanging liquid dollar liabilities to foreigners. In December 1972 we had a total of some $83 billion such liquid liabilities, of which more than $61 billion were owed to foreign official institutions. Somehow or other we must arrange to consolidate these liquid or short-term liabilities into long-term debt. Apart from this, our principal interim policy should be, of course, to stop increasing the supply of paper money and bank credit.

As long, however, as we and the rest of the world are on a mere paper money basis, we should not try to maintain a fixed rate for the dollar vis-à-vis other currencies. This could only be maintained by government-pegging operations, by swap arrangements, and by government intervention daily in the foreign exchange market to buy and sell other currencies. As long as governments are all inflating at different rates, these pegged rates are bound to break down, with sudden and violent overnight changes jolting to business confidence.

Insofar as the world is on a paper basis, the least objectionable policy is to let the dollar float in the foreign exchange markets. Floating paper currencies, of course, are not a satisfactory solution of anything. There are 120 currencies in the International Monetary Fund. If all float freely, there will be more than 14,000 cross-rates (counting each plus its reciprocal) bouncing around daily and hourly in the foreign exchange markets—hardly an ideal situation. We need at least one constant objective standard of measurement.

Ultimately, the world must return to the gold standard. What does the gold standard mean? It means that any unit of fiduciary currency is convertible on demand into a given weight of gold, and vice versa. In the pre-1914 world each major national currency was in fact convertible on demand into a specific weight of gold. In turn each national currency unit was convertible into any of the others at the proportional rate. Because a pound sterling was convertible into 4.86 times as much gold as an American dollar, the pound was equivalent to $4.86.

There was no formal international covenant, signed by a hundred nations, or even by a Big Twenty or a Big Ten. No formal international agreement was needed. All that was needed was that each country pay its debts and honor its pledges to keep its currency unit convertible into the specific amount of gold it had fixed. As long as each country did this, all currency rates were necessarily fixed in terms of each other.

The only form of international cooperation that is now necessary or desirable, once we readopt a gold standard, is that the relative gold conversion rates fixed by the principal countries be easily translatable into each other in round figures—one to one, two to one, four to one, or, say, one-quarter gram of gold, one-half gram, one gram. In addition, international economic cooperation need consist merely in each nation refraining from protectionism and beggar-my-neighbor policies.

But if we are ultimately to return to a gold standard, we face the delicate question of how we can find, without creating either inflation or deflation, the most suitable and sustainable rate of conversion of the dollar into gold. It can never again be the $20.67 an ounce actually maintained from 1879 to 1933, nor the $35 an ounce nominally maintained from 1934 to 1971, nor the short-lived nominal rate of $38 an ounce established in December 1971; nor can it be the almost purely fictitious $42.22 an ounce ostensibly prevailing today.

We need merely glance at a few current figures. The Treasury's gold stock today, even at a $42.22 an ounce rate, amounts to only some $11 billion. Against this there are outstanding about $258 billion of currency and demand deposits, and some $533 billion if we count time deposits in commercial banks. This means that for every gold dollar in the Treasury there are more than $48 of liquid paper claims. With such a ratio of paper claims to gold, no gold conversion could possibly be sustained, particularly after all the shocks to confidence in their money that Americans have experienced since 1933, and even since 1973.

The most promising procedure would be for our government to allow its citizens to hold gold and to trade in it freely, to keep stringent limits on its increases, if any, in the paper money supply, and to watch at what rate the price of gold tends to stabilize. This could be at best only a provisional guide, because the price of gold in the open market would itself depend to a large extent on what speculators (which potentially includes all of us) thought the government was eventually going to do.

There would be further problems in choosing a "correct" gold conversion rate, which it would be premature to try to deal with in detail here. One point I would like to make emphatically now, however, is that during this floating paper dollar period, the U.S. government should itself neither buy nor sell gold, but simply hold on to its present stock.

I come finally to the question of what type of gold standard the United States should attempt to return to. And here, I am afraid, I shall have to differ with many of my friends who share my belief in a gold standard but who would be content to return to, say, the Federal Reserve System as it functioned from 1914 to 1933. I must say in all candor that I have come to have the gravest doubts about the Federal Reserve System. It seems to me that like the IMF the Federal Reserve has served mainly as an inflation factory. I have come to have the gravest doubts, in fact, about the wisdom of central banks anywhere, and, going further, even about the whole fractional reserve system. By its alternate expansions and contractions of the money supply, it tends to breed booms followed by credit crises, panics, and depressions. We could not return today to a

"pure" gold standard, of course, without an intolerable contraction of the money supply, but we could return to a system
which locks the paper money and credit supply just where it is.

However, this brings us to a subject so large that it could
itself occupy a full lecture—or a full book—or a full library. All
this is premature. I am afraid that in the present atmosphere
even the immediate and interim steps I have been suggesting
will sound wildly unrealistic.

The nations of the world are not only inflating as never
before; they are drenched in an ideology of inflation. Nearly
everybody in official circles in every country now seems to
believe that continuous and perhaps even accelerated inflation
is necessary to maintain "full employment" and "economic
growth." As long as this inflation ideology prevails, I see no
possibility of returning to a sound currency anywhere. Nor can
I even see what, short of some crisis or crack-up that I do not
like to contemplate, will finally bring this worldwide inflationary mania to an end.

5

The Legal Standing of Gold— Contract vs. Status

JOHN A. SPARKS

Associate Professor of Economics, Hillsdale College

"FROM STATUS TO CONTRACT"

Sir Henry Maine, English historian and lawyer, said in his book, *Ancient Law*: "The movement of the progressive societies has hitherto been a movement from status to contract."[1] Maine is well known for his contrast of a "status" society with a "contractual" one. His observation provides the general framework for our analysis of the legal standing of monetary gold today.

The Status Society

Status has been defined as "a legal, personal relationship, not temporary in its nature nor terminable at the mere will of the parties, with which third persons and *the state are concerned.*"[2] [emphasis mine] F.A. Hayek described status as "an assigned place that each individual occupies in society," because of the conference of "special rights and duties" by the state upon some and not others.[3] These definitions describe status as:

1. a fixed relationship which is not terminable, between persons in a society, and

2. a condition conferred by a governmental agency —the state—or a person with quasi-governmental authority.

Historically, the best example of a status society is medieval feudalism. As early as the middle of the sixth century its basic outlines were discernible. Proto-feudalism, that is, an incipient status system, existed in Europe because of the breakdown of the Roman Empire. "In these lawless times, the weak were forced to seek the assistance of the strong, who furnished them with protection and sustinence."[4] The creation of numerous lord-vassal relationships set the stage for formal, fully developed feudalism in which the lord held large amounts of quasi-governmental power over tenants under him. Each man's place or position depended on his relation to the lord. "Divisions within society . . . were established or protected by law . . . one was born into a particular class and might be expected to remain in that class for the whole of his life."[5] *Feudalism was truly a status society.*

The Emergence of a Contract Society

The history of the late Middle Ages illustrates the movement from a status society to a contractual society. In England, for example, formal feudalism (which had been imported by William in 1066) began to change. In the thirteenth and fourteenth centuries, lords began to hire labor for cash rather than rely upon the labor of their villeins (serfs).[6] Though it may not seem important, this process of hiring tenants was significant. Distinctly contractual relations were being established. At the same time the town merchants were gaining greater contractual freedom.[7] Transactions within the towns were often released from the lord's control by special charters. Within the town's boundaries a kind of freedom to hold markets and fairs existed. By the fifteenth century, the old status-nobility had been divested of much of its power by wealthy merchants who had attained their place largely by *contractual activities.*[8]

The Contractual Society

A contract society had begun to emerge, although an intermediate "system" existed for several centuries which was neither feudalistic nor fully contractual. Under mercantilism, as it came to be called, the post-medieval state intervened in contractual dealings through elaborate commercial regulations, control of precious metals, restrictions on trade, and preoccupation with the balance of payments. But, in the eighteenth century, the contractual society become fully developed. It differed in many fundamental legal respects from the status society which preceded it.

First, relationships were created one to another by mutual assent. Second, these ties were more temporary than the interminable status ties. A contract between two parties was likely to run only a short time before the performance of the parties discharged them from further obligation. Third, and most important, *the state became only incidental to the contract.* Government was not responsible for creating the contractual relationship. As it is said: "Contracts receive legal sanction from the agreement of the parties."[9] The state's function is merely to enforce the wills of the parties if one or the other should balk at doing what he had earlier agreed to do. As Hayek said, the contract is the "instrument that the law supplies to the individual to shape his own position."[10] "Status to contract" as it is being used here means the enlargement of the sphere open to the individual for the creation of voluntary relationships with his fellow men. By contrast, the citizen of a status society finds himself immobilized by legally created and maintained restrictions.

Contract and Money

Accompanying and complementing the emergence of the contract society is the *sine qua non* of promissory relationships—money. The contract-exchange society is unthinkable without a medium to facilitate transactions. Money and contract are like two good friends—wherever one is found, one finds the other. By contrast, the decreased use of money forebodes the decline of contract. The disappearance of Roman gold coins in many parts of Roman and barbarian Europe by the end of Justinian's reign was a prelude to the relapse of Europe into the primitive local economies of feudalism.[11]

The complementary and inseparable nature of contract and money was recognized in our own constitution. The Founders, in an effort to promote the benefits of a contractual society, set out to protect the medium which facilitated contracts—gold and other money metals. The constitutional protections that the Founders afforded to money metal are discussed below.

THE CONSTITUTION—GUARDIAN OF GOLD

In General

The U.S. Constitution was originally designed to promote

the contractual society. Obvious provisions come to mind: states are forbidden to impair contract obligations[12]; no express power is granted to the United States to deal with contracts; real and personal property, the fruits of contracts, are specifically protected.[13]

Some of these provisions, along with others, were also clearly intended to promote the contractual society *by protecting the medium of exchange*—monetary gold and other money metals. Rights to money were intended to be sustained in three ways:

1. The integrity of gold and silver coin was to be protected.

2. The individual citizen's right to specify what shall be the medium of exchange in a contract was to be protected.

3. The retention of money metal in the cash holdings of individual citizens was to be protected.

The Coinage Clause

Understanding the "coinage clause" in Article I, § 8 of the Constitution is the starting point for grasping the Founding Fathers' conception of money. By that provision, the Constitution gives Congress the power "to coin money, regulate the value thereof, and of foreign coin, and to fix the standard of weights and measures."[14] Except for some differences in other regards, the power to coin is taken from a similar provision in the Articles of Confederation. Under the Articles, the Continental Congress was given two limited powers. One was to regulate "the alloy," that is, what portion of the coin shall be valuable money metal and what portion shall be baser metal. The other function was to fix the value of the coin by determining the total weight of the money metal contained in it compared to other coins.[15] During 1785 and 1786, proposals suggesting various weights and alloys came forth. The Congress took action on one proposal, but the act never became fully operative.[16]

Eventually, the power to set the weight or value and alloy appeared as the coinage provision of the new Constitution of 1787. By 1792, the young U.S. Congress had set the weight of gold, silver, and copper coins.[17] Thereafter, U.S. citizens, upon entering a contract, knew that their insistence on payment in "dollars" meant that they would be entitled to receive so many ounces of gold or silver. *The "dollar" was really a word which described a unit of weight.* The government's role was limited to that of assaying the money metal and stamping it into coins which would be identifiable as containing a certain quantity of gold or silver.

There is further textual evidence that this was the intent of the writers of the Constitution. Included in the coinage clause, and only set apart by a comma, is the charge "to fix the standard of weights and measures." The juxtaposition of the two powers is commented on in *The Federalist*: "The regulation of weights and measures . . . is founded on like considerations with the preceding power of regulating coin."[18] Fixing the number of inches in a foot and determining how many grains of gold were to be in a "dollar" were similar functions. Thus, similar powers granted in the Articles, *The Federalist* commentary, and the logic of construction, all indicate that the power to coin money and regulate its value was limited to the guaranteeing of the weight and fineness of coins in circulation. Governmental minting was an anti-fraud device designed to promote safer contractual exchange.

No less an economist than Ludwig von Mises has supported the traditional prerogative of state mintage in the *limited sense* prescribed by the U.S. Constitution. He says in *The Theory of Money and Credit*:

> . . . the whole aim and intent of state intervention in the monetary sphere is simply to release individuals from the

necessity of testing the weight and fineness of gold they receive, a task which can only be undertaken by experts and which involves very elaborate precautionary measures. The narrowness of the limits within which the weight and fineness of the coins is legally allowed to vary at the time of minting, and the establishment of a further limit to the permissible loss by wear of those in circulation, is a much better means of securing the integrity of the coinage than the use of scales and nitric acid on the part of all who have commerical dealings.[19]

Elsewhere in the same volume, Mises reiterates that manufacturing coins with similarity of appearance, weight, and fineness "was and still is the premier task of state monetary activity."[20]

It is not necessary to our argument here that the author be entirely satisfied with the sagacity of the "coinage clause." Dr. Hans Sennholz and Dr. Murray Rothbard have both pointed out the desirability of private mintage.[21] As an anti-fraud device, private minting and testing may be preferable to a government mint. Nevertheless, the coinage clause did give the U.S. government the *limited* power to protect the integrity of coined money metal. Mises states that there have been governments which "considered the manufacturing of coins not as a source of surreptitious fiscal lucre but as a public service designed to safeguard a smooth functioning of the market."[22] Mises' statement captures the intent of the Founders.

Money and Constitutional Contract Protection

The Constitution, as ratified, protected the freedom to use money metal such as gold in all exchanges. Contractual rights included the right to exchange one's goods and services for gold or to exchange one's gold for someone else's goods and services. In fact, during and after the Civil War, contracts, especially long-term obligations, contained "gold clauses" which specified that payment was to be made in gold coin or in other money equal in value to a certain weight of gold.[23] Such contract clauses were designed to protect the parties to the contract from unbargained for gains or losses due to the depreciation of the currency (U.S. notes or "greenbacks") then being circulated.

The constitutional protections afforded contracts are unambiguous. First, the states are expressly prohibited from passing any law impairing the obligation of contracts.[24] No state may, in effect, say to a party, "You shall be discharged from your contractual obligation by doing something other than you agreed to do." Experience with the states during the preconstitutional period actually accounts for the prohibition. Justice Story in his *Commentaries on the Constitution* describes the kinds of laws passed by various states which altered the performance of one of the parties.[25] There were laws declaring state-issued money and all sorts of real and personal property legal tender. There were appraisement laws which fixed outlandishly high values on property sought by a creditor and installment laws which put off the payment of the debt past its originally-agreed-upon due date. Finally, there were laws suspending debts altogether. In short, almost any piece of legislation which one might imagine to impair contracts existed in one state or another. Since the states had abused contract rights so consistently, the Founders negated any question that might have existed on the matter by enjoining them from such actions.

The constitutional injunction against the states was plain to see, but, did it apply to a federal law impairing contract? It is true that no specific prohibition exists upon the powers of Congress to impair contracts. But outright prohibition is not the only way in which the Founders restricted the powers of Congress. In addition to outright prohibitions, the framers of the Constitution relied upon the doctrine of delegated powers. The newly created government was to be one of specifically granted or delegated powers. The powers which the new government possessed were limited to those given to it by the Constitution.[26] The negative implication of the doctrine was that those powers not given to the new central government resided elsewhere, either in the states, or if not there, in the people. Article X contains the reasoning in a nutshell: "The powers not delegated to the United States by the Constitution, nor prohibited by it to the states, are reserved to the states respectively, or to the people." One searches in vain to find any specifically delegated power to impair contracts. And, since that power is specifically denied the states, it resides in no governmental body, but remains with the people.

In summary, if parties to a contract designate payment in money metal or use a term which stands for a certain quantity of money metal (such as dollar), then neither the state nor the federal government has any delegated authority to impair the obligation created.

Money as Property Under the Due Process Clauses of the Fifth and Fourteenth Amendments

Ownership has been described as a "bundle of rights" which includes the right to possess, use, receive income from, alienate (transfer title to), and devise tangible or intangible property. Under the Fifth and Fourteenth Amendments to the Constitution, both the federal government and the states are denied the right to deprive persons of life, liberty, and *property* without due process of law. The Founders provided protection for all property and, since gold and other money metals qualify as items of property, they too are protected.

The "due process of law" concept has been traced as far back as the Magna Carta,[27] where it originally operated as a limitation on legislative powers by placing certain procedures beyond the reach of lawmakers.[28] But, as Mussatti has pointed out, "due process of law" means something more than a set procedure. The essence of due process is "substantive due process," that is, "a fair procedure *where the law is interpreted in keeping with constitutional limitations.*"[29] Corwin shows that as early as 1857 in the Dred Scott case the Supreme Court interpreted the Fifth Amendment to prohibit the denial of property because such a denial was substantively prohibited, not because the procedure for enforcing the act in question was improper.[30] In several cases over the next eight decades the Supreme Court struck down various attempts to regulate the economy under the due process clauses of the Fifth and Fourteenth Amendments.[31] Therefore, until the 1930s the fact that a law was passed or a procedure established was not enough to satisfy the due process requirement. Interference with property could not exceed constitutional limits.

Furthermore, when private property was taken under procedures which were fair and under powers properly granted to the government, the Constitution ordered a "just compensation" to be paid. The determination of just compensation was to be made in such a way that the owner had an opportunity to be heard.

In summary, the protection against the taking of one's property was procedural and substantial. After those hurdles, if property was constitutionally available, remuneration had to be paid for it. Personal and real property, including gold and other money metals, was well protected by the Constitution.

THE CONSTITUTION PERVERTED

In General

Over nearly 200 years, the pro-contract thrust of the Constitution has been whittled away bit by bit. Those portions reviewed above, which protected ownership and exchange of money metal, have fared very badly. Executive orders, legislative enactments, and court interpretations, running contrary to the concepts of property in money, contract in money, and integrity in coinage, have become commonly accepted.

Witness the position of gold in the United States from 1933 to 1974.

With minor exceptions, the yellow metal could not be freely acquired, held, imported, or exported. Practically speaking, no private, domestic, or international transactions were legally sanctioned in gold. Gold payments could not be insisted upon by parties to a private contract. Gold could not be coined, nor was it, for much of the period, backing for circulating paper media. From 1971 on, gold was not payable in settlement of international debt.

There is neither space nor need to trace historically the demise of the gold coin standard. It is more important to explore the legal arguments which have so completely undermined the pro-contract, pro-money provisions of the Constitution. A lasting restoration of the gold standard will not be possible unless the constitutional protections guaranteeing such a standard are revived and the arguments against those protections are repudiated.

The Legal Tender Cases

The exigencies of the Civil War soon created an important break in the constitutional armor that surrounded money metal. On February 25, 1862, Congress authorized the issuance of United States notes (greenbacks) to be lawful money and legal tender for all debts public and private. There was no precedent for such a designation. Other similar acts soon followed. The whole matter provoked heated debate. Even supporters of the legal tender issuance argued that such a measure was only justified, given the grave state of the Union.[32] Secretary of Treasury Chase said that he felt "a great aversion to making anything but coin a legal tender in payment of debts."[33] After the end of the war, disputes arose concerning the questions of specie resumption and note retirement. As a result, a group of cases was appealed to the U.S. Supreme Court questioning the constitutionality of the Civil War legislation. The "Legal Tender Cases,"[34] as they came to be called, deserve to be read carefully by political economists and lawyers. (Unfortunately, most recent constitutional law casebooks do not include the opinions.) They contain the fundamental arguments which eroded the protections for sound money as well as vigorous defenses of the right to hold money metal.

In *Knox v. Lee*, one of the Legal Tender Cases, Mr. Justice Strong set forth the reasoning by which the court concluded that the Legal Tender Acts were constitutional. Though one might expect the main argument to be that the power to make notes legal tender was auxiliary to an express power—probably the power to coin money—this was not the case. Given the constitutional atmosphere then prevailing, such an argument based on the "power to coin" would have been regarded as an unwarranted expansion of that clause. The power to establish a mint, for example, might be "necessary and proper" to the express coinage power, but the issuing of legal tender notes certainly was not considered to be so. Consequently, Mr. Justice Strong and the legal tender majority relied upon an argument called "the resulting powers doctrine."

It was certain, the reasoning went, that the United States had been given the power to levy taxes, coin money, raise and support an army and navy, and that these powers were given to establish a sovereign government "with the capability of self-preservation."[35] The derivation of authority from a single enumerated power was unnecessary to sustain an act of Congress. Powers did exist that were neither expressly given nor implied from any single power. Powers of this sort were resulting powers and arose from the sum of the powers of government. Justice Strong concluded that the legal tender enactments were based on properly exercised resulting powers.

The resulting powers doctrine was used to justify further strengthening of the government's control of money. In *Julliard v. Greenman*,[36] the doctrine served as the basis for the conclusion that the legal tender power was not just a war emergency power but a regular peacetime power as well. Much later, in the Gold Clause Cases, the Supreme Court relied upon a "broad and comprehensive national authority over the subjects of revenue, finance and currency . . . derived from the aggregate of the powers granted to the Congress embracing the powers to lay and collect taxes, to borrow money, to regulate commerce . . . to coin money. . . ."[37]

However, the Legal Tender Cases contain more than arguments about resulting powers. The pro-legal tender Justices had to deal with specific constitutional provisions opposing the Legal Tender Acts. The objections had been eloquently raised by Chief Justice Chase in the first Legal Tender Case (*Hepburn v. Griswold*) where the court had found the acts unconstitutional.

The Constitution, Chase had said, prohibited the state legislatures from passing any laws impairing the obligation of contracts. Further, by refusing to grant such a power to the federal Congress, the Founders assumed that no such authority would be exercised by that body either.[38] Also, added Chase, the Fifth Amendment forbade the taking of property without due process of law. Contracts were property, and clearly contracts were being impaired and property improperly taken when debts and obligations were diminished in value.[39]

Justice Strong attempted to counter Chase's assertions. Whenever Congress passes a bankruptcy act or declares war, claimed Strong, many contracts are impaired and a great deal of property is taken with the mere flourish of the legislative pen. If such acts are constitutional, then the fact that contracts are impaired and property taken by the enactment of legal tender laws is just another case where the power of Congress may be exerted for a legitimate purpose, but in the process annul or impair contracts.[40]

Chase's rejoinder was that the power to declare war and to make uniform bankruptcy laws were examples of *expressly delegated powers*. He was not claiming, he said, that "a law made in execution of any other express power, which, incidentally only, impaired the obligation of a contract can be held to be unconstitutional for that reason." But the Constitution grants no express power, nor does it, properly understood, allow any implied power to issue legal tender notes.[41]

Despite Chase's strict constitutional arguments, the Legal Tender Cases upheld the power of Congress to make the United States notes legal tender for all debts public and private. Fortunately, cases decided in 1868 and 1872[42] construed the Legal Tender Acts as *not* applying to contracts in which payment was *expressly* limited to gold coins. Therefore, a dual system of gold and legal tender notes continued.[43] Even though gold could still be insisted upon in exchange, dangerous precedents had been set. It has been observed: "How irresistible a force is faulty precedent, exception becomes the rule . . . if a stand ever is to be made, it must be at the outset. Once the dike of constitutional guarantees is out, innovation pours through without interruption."[44] The dike was broken.

The Federal Reserve System

During the period between the Legal Tender Cases and the New Deal, the weakening of protections for property and contracts was occurring in ways too numerous to explore within the confines of this paper.[45] These changes were to surface dramatically in 1933 and 1934. However, attention will now be directed to establishment of the Federal Reserve System in 1914.

The Federal Reserve Act of 1914 presented no constitutional problem to legal commentators. Most had conceded the position of *McCulloch v. Maryland*[46] where Justice Marshall asserted that the establishment of a national bank was legitimately derived from the power to coin and borrow money. Although challenges to the Federal Deposit Insurance Corporation[47] and the provision permitting state banks to become members of the Federal Reserve System[48] have been unsuccessfully made, no constitutional challenge to the act as a whole has been made.[49]

Despite the unfortunate centralization of banking which later made government controls on money simpler to administer, the enactment of the Federal Reserve Act did not eliminate the use of gold bullion and coin. Bakewell points out: "Under the act [Federal Reserve Act] . . . the basic banking asset continued to be gold, which was our coin and our standard of value, and in which all currency could be redeemed upon demand. The Federal Reserve Act itself said that nothing in it repealed the law of 1900 [Gold Standard Act]."[50] Contractual dealings using gold money would last for two decades after its enactment.

There was reason for concern, from a legal standpoint, about another aspect of the Federal Reserve Act. A large portion of the expanded power of Congress over banking and money was delegated by the legislation to a quasi-governmental entity, the Federal Reserve Board. Initially, the delegation of the monetary powers did not seem so important, for the reserve system was "established when the gold standard ruled supreme."[51] It was the requirement of gold reserves which was regarded as the continuing check on an unwarranted increase in the supply of money, not the Federal Reserve Board. However, as the gold standard was gradually abandoned worldwide and finally domestically, the discretionary control which had been vested in the Federal Reserve became, by default, a substitute for the regulation of the gold standard. As history has proven, it has been a poor substitute.

The way was now paved for the complete demise of gold. Governmental power over money matters had been greatly expanded and then delegated to an independent agency removed from the control of the citizenry.

1933 TO THE PRESENT—THE DEMISE OF GOLD

Rothbard is correct when he says that the abandonment of the gold standard worldwide from 1931 to 1933 "was not a sudden shift from gold weight to paper name; it was but the last step in a lengthy complex process."[52] The death knell for constitutional protections of monetary gold rang in the distance until 1933. There was no mistaking its peal after that year.

Only two days after taking office, President Roosevelt issued an executive order in which he proclaimed a three-day "bank holiday."[53] He relied for such powers on a 1917 war enactment called the Trading With the Enemy Act.[54] Section 5(b) of that act had given wartime President Wilson the power to "investigate, regulate, or prohibit . . . any transactions in foreign exchange and the export, hoarding, melting or earmarking of gold or silver coin or bullion or currency." The rather heavy maximum penalty prescribed by the wartime measure was to be applied to all violators of the President's executive order —namely, a fine of up to $10,000 and, for natural persons, up to ten years of imprisonment or both. On March 9, 1933, the earlier order was extended "until further proclamation by the President."[55] On the same day the Congress approved and confirmed the President's action by passing the "Emergency Banking Act."[56] That act amended the Trading With the Enemy Act so as to give the President the power to prohibit gold hoarding, melting, or export "during time of war or during *any other period of national emergency declared by the President* [emphasis mine]."[57] Perhaps, the most portentous part of the emergency legislation was the addition of Section 11(n) to the Federal Reserve Act, which granted the Secretary of the Treasury the power to protect the currency system of the United States by requiring "all individuals, partnerships . . . and corporations to . . . deliver" to the Treasurer of the United States "any and all gold coin, gold bullion, and gold certificates owned" by them. Ironically, in order to "protect the currency" U.S. citizens could be ordered by the government to relinquish money metal and claims to money metal. The Emergency Banking Act went on to promise that *should such action be necessary*, the Secretary of the Treasury would pay for the gold, but only in *"any other form of coin or currency coined or issued under the laws of the United States* [emphasis mine]."[58]

In less than a month, Roosevelt issued another executive order which required "all persons . . . to deliver . . . to a Federal Reserve Bank . . . all the gold coin, gold bullion, and gold certificates . . ." which they then owned.[59] There were some minor exceptions.[60] Member Federal Reserve Banks who were to receive this gold were merely conduits. Gold deposited with them had to be turned over to Federal Reserve District Banks.[61] If that was not enough, Congress gave further power to the President by passing an amendment to the Agricultural Adjustment Act, called the Thomas Amendment.[62] The amendment allowed for note issuance up to $3 billion and a proclamation by the President reducing the gold content of the dollar by no more than half.

Private and public contracts still contained provisions calling for payment in gold or its equivalent in value. Many contracts and "almost all bonds" public or private contained gold clauses in 1933.[63] "Gold Clauses" were nullified by a Joint Congressional Resolution which claimed that the clauses obstructed the power of Congress to regulate the value of money and keep every dollar of equal value.[64] Therefore, "every provision contained in or made with respect to any obligation which purports to give the obligee a right to require payment in gold . . . is declared to be against public policy. . . . Every obligation, heretofore or hereafter incurred . . . shall be discharged upon payment, dollar for dollar, in any coin or currency which at the time of payment is legal tender for public and private debts."[65]

Another executive order followed[66] and on January 15, 1934, the President requested new legislation to "organize a currency system that will be both sound and adequate."[67] He said in part:

> . . . the free circulation of gold coins is unnecessary, leads to hoarding, and tends to a possible weakening of national financial structures in times of emergency. The practice of transferring gold from one individual to another or from the government to an individual within a Nation is not only unnecessary, but is in every way undesirable . . . Therefore it is a prudent step to vest in the government of a Nation the title to and possession of all monetary gold within its boundaries and to keep that gold in the form of bullion rather than in coin.[68]

Congress responded to the President's request by passing the Gold Reserve Act of 1934.[69] All gold coin and bullion held by Federal Reserve Banks were to pass to the U.S. government.[70] Under the act every Federal Reserve Bank had to maintain certain reserves: gold certificates or lawful money of not less than 35 percent of deposits and gold certificates of not less than 40 percent of Federal Reserve notes in circulation.[71] Section 5 of the Gold Reserve Act eliminated gold coinage and Section 6 proclaimed that except when allowed by regulations issued by the Treasury with presidential approval, "No currency of the United States shall be redeemed in gold. . . ." In Section 12 of the Gold Reserve Act Congress declared that the weight of the gold dollar could not be fixed any higher than 60 percent of its existing weight. The following day, January 31, 1934, Roosevelt reduced the gold content of the dollar by executive order from 25.8 grains,* nine-tenths fine, to 15 5/21 grains, nine-tenths fine.[72] This was a reduction in the gold content of the dollar to about 59 percent of its former value.

In less than a year's time the acquisition, holding, exporting, and earmarking of gold had been eliminated with a few minor exceptions. Domestic convertibility of paper money to gold had been abandoned. The gold content of the dollar for

---

*25.8 grains was the content originally designated by the Gold Standard Act of 1900 (31 Stat. L. 451).

purposes of foreign settlements had been reduced by 40 percent. Gold in the hands of the public had been nationalized.

The constitutionality of the Joint Congressional Resolution abrogating the gold clauses in private contracts came before the Supreme Court in 1935.[73] The opinion written by Chief Justice Hughes disregarded the sanctity of private contracts and relegated them to a position of inferiority.

In the contract at issue in the suit, the parties had agreed that the principal and the interest payments would be made ". . . in gold coin of the United States of America of or equal to the standard weight and fineness existing on February 1, 1930."[74] First, the court interpreted the contract as requiring payment in "money," not in bullion or coin.[75] After referring frequently to the Legal Tender Cases, the opinion continued: "Contracts may create rights of property, but when contracts deal with a subject matter which lies within the control of Congress, they have a congenital infirmity. Parties cannot remove their transactions from the reach of dominant constitutional power by making contracts about them. . . . If the gold clauses now before us interfere with the policy of the Congress in the exercise of [constitutional] . . . authority they cannot stand."[76] By a margin of five to four the court found that they did interfere and that Congress acted within its legitimate authority. (The arguments which dispute that position were made earlier in this paper.) Associate Justice McReynolds summed it up when he reportedly blurted to the packed courtroom: "As for the Constitution, it does not seem too much to say that it is gone."[77]

By legislation enacted in 1945,[78] 1965,[79] and 1968,[80] Congress demonetized gold domestically. President Nixon's suspension of international gold payments in August 1971 resulted in a complete fiat standard.

From 1934 to 1974 American citizens had no full ownership rights with respect to holding or exchanging gold. Instead they had, at best, residuary rights, which were enumerated in the "Gold Regulations," a seventeen-page booklet of rules issued by the Department of the Treasury. Legal gold ownership[81] was possible only to the extent permitted by the gold regulations and the licenses issued thereunder.[82] The only exceptions which allowed some interest in gold to be held by citizens were the "rare coin," "customary use," and gold-mining share exceptions.[83]

One could acquire, hold, and exchange gold coins of recognized value to collectors without a license.[84] One could apply for a license to make a legitimate and customary use of gold in an industry, profession, or art.[85] The holding of gold mining shares was not prohibited.[86] However, the ordinary citizen who wanted to purchase bullion and hold it or use it in exchange could not do so.*

Under an amendment to the International Development Association (IDA) bill, to become effective December 31, 1974, U.S. citizens are, once again, allowed to buy and sell gold bullion.[87] What appears to be the restoration of fundamental contract and property rights may be something less than that, however. First, the authority to accord citizens the right to own gold is now clearly viewed as a legislative prerogative. Moreover, it is unfortunately true that an "emergency" declared by the executive could once again result in restriction on gold ownership.

Secondly, while the privilege to buy and sell gold as a commodity is granted by the legislation, the legality of gold clauses in contracts is still uncertain. As a recent article in the *American Bar Association Journal* has pointed out, there are practical problems with gold clauses, involving tax considerations, usury laws, specific performance and negotiabili-

---

*There exists a low-level federal court case where the defendants successfully challenged the criminal provisions of the law. In a 1962 District Court decision, Southern District of California Judge William C. Mathes dismissed criminal charges against two defendants who owned gold bullion. Unfortunately, the decision is of little value as a precedent and says nothing of the civil penalties that require forfeiture and a penalty payment.

ty.[88] But the central question concerns the legal status of gold ownership in the light of the gold clause cases referred to above: "In view of the involved reasoning of the Gold Clause Cases . . . it is possible that the Supreme Court, on some theory, might hold that the use of gold clauses would still be ineffective, even after our right to hold gold has been restored."[89] Barring favorable judicial construction, the "gold ownership" privilege established by recent legislation is but a shadow of the full-fledged, pre-1934 right of ownership.

WHICH WAY: STATUS TO CONTRACT OR THE REVERSE?

Maine's observation of the movement from "status to contract" rings hollow in the face of the astounding anti-contractualism of our day. Instead of promoting contracts by maintaining the integrity of the medium of exchange, the state has engaged in sophisticated coin clipping. Instead of the right to make contracts which specify gold as the medium of the exchange, citizens must rely on various complicated strategems to compensate for the instability of fiat currency. Instead of the right to retain money metal in one's cash holdings, one must venture into the fields of numismatics, gold mining shares, real property investment, or some other indirect hedge against monetary depreciation. These occurrences have made some contracts impossible to enter into and have made all contractual dealings difficult and roundabout. There is no doubt that the sphere of contract has declined. But to assert that there has been a decline of contractualism is one thing; to suggest that there has been a movement toward a status society is another.

It is the historian's province to make final determinations on these matters. And, let it be clear that it is not contended here that a neo-feudal-status society exists or is over the horizon. But a case can be made that elements of a new mercantilism have been becoming more obvious. It is interesting that, historically, mercantilism was the intermediate stage between the status society and the contract society. It is reasonable to assume that a society moving away from contract and back toward status might have neo-mercantilistic characteristics.

Two decades ago Rogge and Van Sickle claimed: "Today we are far closer to 18th century mercantilism than to 19th century liberalism. National state planning is again in vogue. Production and trade are highly regulated . . . national economic policies are, in fact, dominated by the same balance of payments preoccupations that inspired so much of the planning of the age of mercantilism."[90] About the same time Ballvé said that "exacerbated nationalism" and "socialism" and "distrust of individual initiative" had combined "at the end of the nineteenth century and the beginning of the twentieth in *neomercantilism.*"[91] Certainly, circumstances have become more mercantile since these observations. Barriers to trade, domestic and international regulation of foreign exchange, legislation to encourage exports and discourage imports, and bills to erect further barriers in the offing do not indicate a decline of neo-mercantilist influence.

Recently, Sennholz once again warned of the prospects of further disintegration of international trade and finance due to the abandonment of sound monetary policies. He foresaw more neo-mercantilism such as foreign exchange controls, multiple exchange rates, and disruption of world economic relations unless nations altered their current courses.[92] The decline of sound money has bolstered the movement away from contract, but the trend is reversible. It is the reestablishment of proper protections for the gold standard which will once again impel us toward a contractual society.

NOTES

[1]Sir Henry Maine, *Ancient Law* (London: Dent and Sons, 1917), p. 100.

[2]*Holzer v. Deutsche Reichsbahn-Gesellschaft*, 159 Misc. 830, 290 N.Y.S. 181, 191.

[3]F. A. Hayek, *The Constitution of Liberty* (Chicago: The University of Chicago Press, 1960), p. 154.

[4]Archibald R. Lewis, *Emerging Medieval Europe* (New York: Knopf, 1967), p. 24.

[5]Clarence A. Carson, *The Flight from Reality* (New York: The Foundation for Economic Education, Inc., 1969), p. 336.

[6]W. E. Lunt, *History of England* (New York: Harper & Row, Publishers, 1957; 4th ed.), p. 176.

[7]Ibid., pp. 237, 246.

[8]Lunt, *History of England*, p. 289.

[9]"Contractus legem ex combentione accipiunt," *Digest of Justinian*, 16, 3, 1, 6, in Henry C. Black, ed., *Law Dictionary* (St. Paul, Minn.: West Publishing Co., 1957), p. 398.

[10]Hayek, *Constitution of Liberty*, p. 154.

[11]Lewis, *Emerging Medieval Europe*, pp. 17, 20.

[12]U.S. Constitution, Article I & 10.

[13]U.S. Constitution, Amendment V and XIV, Sec. 1. It is interesting to note that the states and the United States are forbidden to create legal classes—the basis for the status society. U.S. Constitution, Article I, Sec. 9 and 10.

[14]U.S. Constitution, Article I & 8.

[15]Articles of Confederation, Article XI.

[16]A. Barton Hepburn, *A History of Currency in the United States* (New York: The Macmillan Co., 1924, revised ed.; reprint, Augustus M. Kelley, Publishers, 1967).

[17]Ibid., p. 43.

[18]*The Federalist* (New York: Wiley Book Co., 1901), XLI, 233.

[19]Ludwig von Mises, *The Theory of Money and Credit* (New Haven: Yale University Press, 1953), pp. 66-67. See also *Human Action* (New Haven: Yale University Press, 1953), pp. 774-776.

[20]Mises, *The Theory of Money and Credit*, p. 71.

[21]Hans Sennholz, *Inflation or Gold Standard?* (Lansing, Mich.:

Bramble Press, 1969), pp. 28-29, and Murray N. Rothbard, "100% Gold Dollar," in Leland B. Yeager, *In Search of a Monetary Constitution* (Cambridge, Mass.: Harvard University Press, 1962).

[22]Mises, *Human Action*, p. 775.

[23]Milton Friedman and Anna J. Schwartz, *A Monetary History of the United States* (Princeton, N. J.: Princeton University Press, 1963), p. 468, 71n.

[24]U.S. Constitution, Article I, Sec. 10.

[25]Joseph Story, *Commentaries on the Constitution*, Sec. 1371, cited in *Julliard v. Greenman*, 110 U.S. 421 (1884), Field's dissenting opinion.

[26]William J. Palmer, *The Courts vs. the People* (Chicago: Chas. Holberg & Co., 1969), p. 68.

[27]See Sir Edward Coke, Institutes, Part 2, cited in Roscoe Pound, *The Development of Constitutional Guarantees of Liberty* (New Haven: Yale University Press, 1957), p. 47.

[28]Edward S. Corwin, *The Constitution, What It Means Today* (Princeton, N. J.: Princeton University Press, 1958), p. 217.

[29]James Mussatti, *The Constitution of the United States* (Princeton, N. J.: D. Van Nostrand, 1958), p. 84.

[30]Corwin, *The Constitution*, p. 218.

[31]See *Lochner v. New York,* 198 U.S. 45, 25 S. Ct. 539, 49 L. Ed. 937 (1905), *Adkins v. Children's Hospital*, 261 U.S. 525, 43 S. Ct. 394, 67 L. Ed. 785 (1923).

[32]Hepburn, *A History of Currency*, pp. 186-190.

[33]Ibid., p. 187. Note that Chase as Chief Justice of the Supreme Court was later to find the Legal Tender Acts, which he himself promoted, unconstitutional.

[34]*Knox v. Lee*, 12 Wall. 457, 20 L. Ed. 287 (1871); *Hepburn v. Griswold*, 8 Wall. 603, 19 L. Ed. 513 (1870); see also *Julliard v. Greenman*, 110 U.S. 421, U.S. Ct., 122, 28 L. Ed. 204 (1884).

[35]*Knox v. Lee*, reprinted in Herman E. Krooss, *A Documentary History of Banking and Currency in the United States* (New York: Chelsea House Publishers, 1969), p. 1555.

[36]*Julliard v. Greenman*, Ohio R.R., 294 U.S. 240, 55 S. Ct. 407, 79 L. Ed. 885 (1935); reprinted in Krooss, *A Documentary History of Banking*, pp. 2848-2849.

[37]*Norman v. Baltimore & Ohio R. R.*, 294 U.S. 240, 55 S. Ct. 432, 79 L. Ed. 912 (1935).

[38]*Hepburn v. Griswold*, reprinted in Krooss, *A Documentary History of Banking*, p. 1533.

[39]Ibid., p. 1541.

[40]*Knox v. Lee*, in Krooss, *A Documentary History of Banking*, p. 1540.

[41]*Hepburn v. Griswold*, in Krooss, *A Documentary History of Banking*, p. 1540.

[42]*Bronson v. Rodes*, 7 Wall. 229, 19 L. Ed. 147, and *Trebilock v. Wilson*, 12 Wall. 687, 20 L. Ed. 460, respectively.

[43]Friedman and Schwartz, *A Monetary History*, p. 15.

[44]Russell Kirk, *John Randolph of Roanoke* (Chicago: Henry Regnery Co., 1964), p. 66.

[45]See Gottfried Dietze, *In Defence of Property* (Chicago: Henry Regnery Co., 1963), Chapters 4, 5, 6.

[46]4 Wheat. 316, 4 L. Ed. 579 (1819).

[47]*Doherty v. U.S.*, C.C.A. Neb. 1938, 94 F. 2d 495, Cert. denied, 58 S. Ct. 763, 303 U.S. 658, 82 L. Ed. 1117.

[48]*Hiatt v. U.S.*, C.C.A. Ind. 1924, 4 F. 2d. 374, Cert. denied, 45 S. Ct. 638, 268 U.S. 704, 69 L. Ed. 1167.

[49]Arthur S. Miller, "Legal View of the Monetary System," in Lewis E. Davids, ed., *Money & Banking Casebook* (Homewood, Ill.: Richard D. Irwin, Inc., 1964), p. 418.

[50]Paul Bakewell, *Inflation in the United States* (Caldwell, Idaho: Caxton Printers, 1958), p. 16. J. D. Paris excludes the Federal Reserve Act from his "Chronology of Important Events Relating to Gold," in *Monetary Policies of the U.S., 1932-38* (New York: Columbia University Press, 1938), p. 118. Perhaps his reasoning follows the analysis of Bakewell.

[51]Milton Friedman, *Dollars & Deficits* (Englewood Cliffs, N.J.: Prentice-Hall, 1968), p. 183.

[52]Murray N. Rothbard, "The Case for a 100 Per Cent Gold Dollar," in Leland B. Yeager, *In Search of a Monetary Constitution* (Cambridge, Mass.: Harvard University Press, 1962), p. 105.

[53]*Public Papers of Franklin D. Roosevelt*, II, 25-29; Krooss, *A Documentary History of Banking*, pp. 2694-2695.

[54]40 Stat. L. 411 (October 6, 1917).

[55]*Public Papers of Franklin D. Roosevelt*, II, 48; Krooss, *A Documentary History of Banking*, p. 2696.

[56]48 Stat. L. 1 (March 9, 1933).

[57]Ibid., Sec. 2.

[58]12 USCA Sec. 248 (n).

[59]Executive Order No. 6102, 31 CFR, 1936 ed., Part 50 (April 5, 1938).

[60]Each person was allowed to keep no more than $100 worth of gold coins and certificates, gold customarily used in a legitimate industry or profession (dentist, jeweler) and gold coins having special value to collectors. Gold coin and bullion earmarked for a foreign government or foreign central bank was not ordered in. Executive Order 6102, Secs. 2(a), 2(b), and 2(c).

[61]Ibid., Sec. 5.

[62]48 Stat. L. 51 (May 12, 1933). Note that twice in 1936 the AAA was held unconstitutional. *Butler v. U.S.*, 296 U.S.1, and *Rice Mills v. Fountenot*, 297 U.S. 110. Finally, in 1939 the act was upheld due to a change in court personnel. *U.S. v. Rock Royal Co.*, 307 U.S. 533. See Lyman A. Garber, *Of Men and Not of Law* (New York: Devin-Adair, 1966), pp. 34-35.

[63]Charles H. Pritchett, *The American Constitution* (New York: McGraw-Hill, 1959), p. 250.

[64]H. J. Res., 192, 73d Cong., 1st Sess. (1933).

[65]Another part of the same resolution abrogated gold clauses in U.S. government obligation.

[66]Executive Order No. 6260, 31 CFR, 1938 ed., Part 50.

[67]*Public Papers of Franklin D. Roosevelt*, III, 40-45; Krooss, *A Documentary History of Banking*, p. 2789.

[68]Krooss, *A Documentary History of Banking*, p. 2790.

[69] 31 USCA 440, 48 Stat. L. 337.

[70]Ibid., Sec. 2(a).

[71]Ibid., Sec. 2(b) 3.

[72]*Public Papers of Franklin D. Roosevelt*, III, 64-66.

[73]*Norman v. Baltimore & Ohio R.R.*, 294 U.S. 240, 55 S. Ct. 407, 79 L. Ed. 885 (1935). See also *Perry v. United States*, 294 U.S. 330, 55 S. Ct. 432, 79 L. Ed. 912 (1935) where the court denied Congress the right to abrogate gold clauses in government obligations *but* then denied the plaintiff recovery because he could show no damage.

[74]*Norman v. Baltimore & Ohio R.R.*, in Charles G. Fenwick, ed., *Cases on American Constitutional Law* (Chicago: Callaghan & Co., 1953), p. 318.

[75]Ibid., p. 320.

[76]Ibid., pp. 321, 322.

[77]Pritchett, *The American Constitution*, p. 250.

[78] 59 Stat. L. 237.

[79] 79 Stat. L. 5.

[80] 12 USCA Sec. 413, 82 Stat. L. 50 (March 18, 1968).

[81]It is estimated that some $287 million in gold was retained illegally in the hands of the public. Friedman and Schwartz, *A Monetary History*, pp. 464-465n.

[82]Gold Regulations Sec. 54.12

[83]Literature is available on gold coin investment and gold mining stock ownership, both of which are legal. See Donald J. Hoppe, *How to Invest in Gold Coins*, and *How to Invest in Gold Stocks* (New Rochelle: Arlington House, 1970 and 1972).

[84]Gold Regulations, Sec. 54.20 as amended.

[85]Gold Regulations, Sec. 54.4(14), 54.22-54.25.

[86]Gold Regulations, Sec. 54.14 (b).

[87]"President Signs Ownership Bill," *Coin Investments Market Letter* 1, no. 19 (August 1974), Coin Investments, Inc., Birmingham, Mich.

[88]Rene A. Wormser and Donald L. Kemmerer. "Restoring 'Gold Clauses' in Contracts," *American Bar Association Journal* 60: 942-946.

[89]Ibid., p. 946.

[90]John V. Van Sickle and Benjamin A. Rogge, *Introductory Economics* (New York: D. Van Nostrand, 1954), p. 543.

[91]Faustino Ballvé, *Essentials of Economics* (New York: The Foundation for Economic Education, 1963), p. 7.

[92]Sennholz, *The Crisis in International Economic Relations* (Hillsdale, Mich.: Hillsdale College, March 1973), 2 *Imprimis*, No. 3.

6

The Role Of Gold
In The Past Century

DONALD L. KEMMERER

Professor of Economics,
University of Illinois

Human experience, as recorded by historians or remembered by man himself, is the laboratory of the social
sciences. That is a major reason for the study of economic and
financial history, which can teach us far more about the
economic behavior of man than can mathematical formulas and
equations. Despite economics' recent romance with mathe-
matics to try to erase the stigma of being an "inexact science," it
remains a social science and remains inexact. Economic
experiments or experiences cannot be controlled the way those
in a chemistry laboratory can. Pour hydrochloric acid over iron
filings and you'll get the same results each time, but "pour" a
sharply increased money supply onto a nation of people and
the immediate results will differ considerably, although higher

prices will almost certainly be the eventual consequence. Mathematical formulas may suggest that a paper money standard is as useful as a gold coin standard, but a study of economic history suggests otherwise.

What does the record of human experience reveal about monetary standards and money? Man has used just about everything one can imagine as money ever since he needed a medium of exchange to make trading easier. Among the items have been beads, pretty seashells, feathers, large stones, tobacco, cattle, iron coins, precious metal coins—the list is a long one. Chase Manhattan Bank of New York has a fascinating money museum with exhibits of many of these and the story of each. Generally, the "money" was something valued for its beauty or its usefulness to nearly everyone, but also it was usually something that man could not quickly produce in great quantity, thus inflating the money supply. The tobacco standard in seventeenth-century Virginia ceased being effective when a large part of the population operated their own mints, i.e., cultivated their fields of tobacco. And modern sea dredging put an end to the cowry shell standard of East African peoples. Over the centuries two products in particular emerged as world favorites, namely gold and silver, and in the last century gold triumphed over silver. True, from about 1690 on, a latecomer standard, fiat paper money, challenged the precious metal standards again and again. Despite fiat money's many disastrous failures, its popularity with governments steadily increased. They never stopped giving it another chance.

The use of gold coins may be traced back to the time of Darius the Great of Persia (521-485 B.C.), but the rules of the modern gold standard have developed only in the last 250 years, starting in 1717 in England. Thanks to the new gold standard Britain had a stable currency in the eighteenth century, despite wars nearly half of the time and bad examples set by her paper-money-minded American colonies and her neighbor, France.

In 1848 gold was discovered in California, leading to the famous Gold Rush of 1849. Similar discoveries and rushes, only slightly smaller, took place in 1851 and 1853 in Australia. One might suppose that the production of gold, even sizable finds of it, would not have a great impact on the accumulation of the ages, for gold is so valuable that once produced it is carefully guarded and little is lost. Yet, between 1850 and 1862, the *monetary* gold of the world doubled and between 1850 and 1875 the world's estimated supply of gold doubled. In general, in the past about half of the gold mined has gone into monetary uses and the rest into ornamentation and other "industrial" uses. Twice since the mid-nineteenth century, the gold stock has again doubled over a relatively short time. Once was in the 1885-1918 period because of Alaskan and South African gold discoveries, plus the introduction of the cyanide process for refining gold. Another was between 1934 and World War II because of the American devaluation of the dollar which raised the price of gold by 69 percent. The same thing could happen again if the present price of gold should remain close to where it is now.

But returning now to the 1850s—because of the scarcity of gold most sound money nations had used two precious metals, gold and silver, a bimetallic standard, until the last third of the nineteenth century. This worked moderately well and would have worked better if the nations had seen the need and had been able to agree on a single value ratio between the two metals before minting their coins. Suffice to say this caused problems and when gold became more plentiful after mid-century, a growing number of countries, taking note of England's long success with the single metal (gold) standard, either shifted to that, or adopted it to begin with if they were stabilizing after a long period of inflation. The shift to gold might have taken place sooner if it had not been for a spate of mid-century wars. Both Austria and Russia sought to return to hard money around 1860, but war and revolution nullified those efforts to stabilize. Civil War in the United States caused us to suspend specie payments for seventeen years (1862-1879), and Prussia's defeat of France in 1870 likewise took France off hard money for about five years. But it may be noted that these countries did not forbid their citizens to own gold or trade in it. The Western world, despite these setbacks, was on the threshold of the great era of the gold coin standard. The success of England's pound set the example, the recent experience some nations had had with inflation (the United States) or floating exchange rates (Italy) provided the incentive, and the discoveries and ensuing enormous production of gold afforded the opportunity. Between 1873 and 1912 the number of primary and secondary nations on the gold standard grew from nine to forty-one.

By this time the definition of a modern gold standard had become fairly clear. It could be described as a money standard in which the unit of value in which prices and wages are customarily expressed was a fixed weight of gold. From this four conclusions followed.

1. There must be free coinage of gold, that is, anyone might bring any amount of gold to the mint to be coined, but not necessarily free of the manufacturing cost of minting the coins.

2. There must be freedom to export or melt down gold coins. That did not, of course, mean freedom to reduce in any way the weight of the coin and then try to pass it on at face value.

3. All moneys of the country, including checking accounts in practice, must be convertible to gold coin.

4. Gold coin must be full legal tender, that is, if a debtor offered to pay his creditor in gold coin and the creditor refused, he could not sue the debtor for nonpayment of the debt.

The monetary unit, the dollar for example, was the value of the stated amount of gold in a free market, and the conditions set forth above ensured that the country itself remained such a free market. If an individual preferred a dollar to 23.22 grains of pure gold, he could convert his gold to a dollar, and if he preferred gold to a dollar, he was free to export or melt his gold coin.

Let us look at the adoption and operation of the new gold standards. Most Americans are familiar with the story of our resumption of specie payments during 1875-1879 after seventeen years on inconvertible paper. Secretary of Treasury Sherman piled up a substantial gold reserve, purposely withheld some greenbacks from circulation, and limited *official* resumption to only one place in the nation, the New York subtreasury. On the fateful day, January 2, 1879, only a few persons presented greenbacks for redemption but many more turned in gold for paper since they felt the paper was now equally safe. It was an anticlimax. From 1896 until the outbreak of World War I the cash reserves against deposits and bank notes of all commercial banks were rarely far off 25 percent, with gold coin and gold certificates sometimes constituting at times as much as about 40 percent of this total.

In Europe where several major nations were returning to gold or making preparations to do so around 1900, finance ministers, central bankers, and bankers showed even greater conservatism. Italy held 60 percent gold reserves in 1903, and on April 11 of that same year the London *Economist* commented, "After the Bank of France, the Austro-Hungarian Banks stands on the broadest base of any note bank in the world." Yet Austria-Hungary, which had made a good partial step toward convertibility in 1901 by issuing gold coins, hesitated to guarantee full convertibility for another decade for fear her gold reserves would not be adequate. But the prize for caution must go to Russia which had over 107 percent gold cover for her notes in 1896 but did not resume specie payments for another year.

I mention all of these, and I might have added others, because they stand in such sharp contrast to Great Britain. With a net national income ranging from $8.3 billion to $9.6 billion between 1901 and 1910, she carried on a merchandise trade of about half that amount each year, easily the world's greatest at the time. This was toward the end of the Boer War (1899-1902), an era of frequent clashes on India's Northwest Frontier, and mounting tensions in Europe. Yet, Britain's bullion reserves against all bank notes and deposits of the nation ranged from 3.5 to 3.9 percent and her *net* exports of bullion in any one year never exceeded $33 million. If there were fears of inadequate liquidity to carry on this enormous trade, they were muted. How did she do it? She had heavy investments overseas earning her citizens substantial profits every year, she carried almost half the world's shipping, and London's "City," or financial center, was the world's most important. Although merchandise imports exceeded merchandise exports every year, the British were living within their income, living off the profits of good investments and not (yet) trying to save the world. All of this gave her pound sterling great credibility. If a currency has that, it does not need a substantial gold backing.

Going back to the 1873-1914 era, a study of resumptions of specie payments is also rewarding. I dug into this subject some years ago because I was unhappy about generalizing from the American experience of 1875-1879 that Amercians know best. Ministers of Finance, Secretaries of the Treasury, leading bankers—in brief those with responsibility for successfully putting their nation back on a gold standard—were, almost to a man, fearful that they did not have enough gold, that a run on their "limited" supply by speculators and others would succeed, humiliate the nation, and damage their own reputations. All of this is understandable. Some of them piled up rather enormous reserves against that "moment of truth," notably in Austria and Russia. But in actual practice the most important ingredients for success were a firm announcement of intention combined with a clearly sincere effort to carry it out. It came down most of all to confidence. Japan had showed her sincerity by minting and issuing gold coin and at the same time withdrawing paper bank notes and silver when she

resumed on October 1, 1897. This courageous effort by her
Finance Minister, Count Matzukata, succeeded despite a
sizably adverse trade balance that year, the onset of a depression, and some erosion of her modest gold reserves. True, the
danger did not end until 1900. Yet once back on a convertible
basis, and with a respectable past, Japan and Russia (she had
also resumed in 1897) fought a costly and bloody war (1904-
1905) without either having to give up their newly acquired
gold standards.

By the end of the nineteenth century, and even earlier, most
of the economically important nations of the world were on a
gold standard. Brazil, China, Spain, and Turkey never made it
but just about all the others did. How well did it work? As the
late Dr. Melchior Palyi states in his posthumous book, *The
Twilight of Gold, 1914-36*: "The gold standard was 'sacrosanct'
to the generations brought up on the Adam Smith ideals of free
markets . . . it was an essential instrument of economic freedom. It protected the individual against arbitrary measures of
the government by offering a convenient hedge against . . . the
depreciation or devaluation of the currency. Above all, it
raised a mighty barrier against authoritarian interferences with
the economic process." (p. 5) And later he adds, "The role of
the gold standard in unifying the economy of the civilized
world can scarcely be overestimated. It was the condition *sine
qua non* of the international capital flow, both short-term and
long-term, a basic instrument in opening up the world to
economic progress and diffusing modern civilization. And the
capital flow under the gold standard operated with a minimum
of actual gold transfers and with modest gold reserves [notably
so for Britain, the great investor]." (p. 9) Along with the gold
standard went the practice of making gold transfers *promptly* if
sufficient payment could not be made by swapping the
proceeds from the international trade of goods and services.
These gold transfers tended to reduce the paying nation's gold
reserves and to result in tighter money and higher interest
rates. If not taken care of promptly, that situation could be

mildly painful but nowhere nearly as painful and humiliating as it would be if ignored or delayed for months or years. But it would leave a mistaken impression to imply that the gold standards were quite automatic and that central bankers or others did not sometimes manage or soften the impact of sizable outflows of gold. For they did, and not always without some deserved penalty. Even so, the system was more automatic in its workings than earlier inconvertible systems had been, and more than our modern ones have been. All is relative.

In the summer of 1914, World War I burst upon the world and destroyed this financial mechanism. The war lasted over four tragic years. From our viewpoint it was the change in attitudes, the bad habits that emerged from those traumatic years, that matter most, although these were not immediately evident. No sooner had the war ended than the major powers resolved to restore the still much esteemed gold standard. International monetary conferences at Brussels in 1920 and at Genoa in 1922 called for restoring it as soon as possible. Even its renowned later opponent, John Maynard Keynes, said in 1922, "If gold standards could be reintroduced throughout Europe, we all agree this would promote, as nothing else can, the revival not only of trade and production, but of international credit and the movement of capital to where it is needed most."

The first major nation to return to a gold standard after World War I was the United States, and it did so simply by removing its embargo on gold exports on June 10, 1919. Lithuania and Costa Rica returned to it in 1922, and before the end of 1923, Austria and Colombia. Sweden, Guatemala, and a chastened Germany (following her horrendous postwar inflation) followed in 1924. If Great Britain's pound sterling was going to regain its prestige once more and if London's financial center was to prosper as before, by 1925 it was high time that Britain return to gold. And if the old image was to be recaptured, then the old 4.86 relationship to the rival dollar had, if at all possible, to be reestablished too. With some effort and mutterings of anxiety among her leaders, Britain did return to a gold bullion standard, and at a 4.86 ratio of the dollar to the pound on April 28, 1925. In 1926 France, too, stabilized her franc. Another nine countries, including Italy and India, followed in 1927. All in all, fifty "nations" returned to gold, the last in July 1931.

Of these fifty countries twelve had a gold coin standard, six a gold bullion standard (most quickly defined as a gold coin standard with the only coin a bar worth, say, $8,000), and the other thirty-two a gold exchange standard. Some of these types were more than a little intermingled, i.e., Holland had coins but also very important deposits in the Bank of England. The gold exchange standard nations relied on the gold bullion standards of Britain and France, or the gold coin standard of the United States. In this country in the 1920s, some 3 percent of the money "in circulation" was still gold coin. But on the whole the nations of the world used gold coin in everyday transactions far more sparingly than before 1914. Increasingly, one heard that there was not enough gold in the world or being produced to service all of these gold standards. Gustav Cassel, Joseph Kitchin, and others voiced this view in widely read books and articles.

Of course, if a nation doubles its money supply, as happened here between 1913 and 1920 (and even after the 1920-1921 depression and adjustment, the price level was 60 percent higher than in 1913) but leaves the price of gold unchanged, it must expect its gold reserves to be relatively scarcer, the mining of gold to be discouraged, and gold's uses for ornamentation to be encouraged at the lower price. To offset this scarcity of gold in the 1910s and 1920s, nations were making their banking systems more efficient and turning to gold standards that economized on the use of gold—not using it for coins, for example.

Still another device, employed in particular in the United States, from about 1922 on was open market operations. They were presumed to be for stifling booms and bringing the country out of a recession. But their use could also delay balance-of-payments adjustments and thus make the gold standard less effective than it had been before 1914. One may well ask whether the long-run effects of this credit control device may have been more harmful than helpful.

Time is far too short to do more than mention the 1929 collapse and the depression that ensued.

In the spring of 1931 Austria's overextended Kredit-Anstalt collapsed, taking that truncated little nation off her gold exchange standard. Panic spread to nearby Germany whose banks had borrowed on short term but loaned on long, and in July she too gave up her tie with gold. The currents of doubt struck at England next. Many felt at the time, and later also, that she defended herself rather ineffectively by not raising her discount rate higher than just 4 1/2 percent. Governor Montagu Norman of the Bank of England, the architect and promoter of many of the world's gold exchange standards, had to be away during the latter part of the crisis because of illness. Before he returned, and much to his displeasure and con-sternation, Britain, too, broke her tie with gold on September 19, 1931. That, of course, swept off the gold standard all those gold exchange standard nations, as well as others who kept substantial reserves in the Bank of England.

The year 1932 was the bottom of the depression. Since the President-elect of the United States was known to be listening to the advice of economists favoring policies that would halt the fall in prices that had been going on since 1929, and might even scrap the gold standard to stop that decline in prices, some anxious individuals, by February 1933, were as worried about the future value of the dollar as they were about the solvency of their banks. Some Americans began hoarding gold. Continued runs on banks culminated in the Bank Holiday at the time of the new President's inauguration (March 4). With that holiday came a temporary embargo on gold exports, then an order forbidding citizens henceforth to buy or own gold coin and to turn in their gold coins and gold certificates to the government.

Finally, on April 20, a more permanent embargo was announced, followed by a drop in dollar exchange. Beyond any remaining doubt the United States had left the gold standard.

Congress gave the new President authority on May 12 to devalue the dollar by as much as 50 percent, institute bimetallism, issue $3 billion in greenbacks, or engage in open market operations to the extent of $3 billion, or any portion or combination of these he might deem desirable. In June the government decreed that the gold clause prevalent in contracts since *Bronson v. Rodes* (1868) would not be respected. In July the United States announced to an International Economic Conference about to be held in London that we would make no agreements with other nations over the extent to which we would devalue the dollar. In October the Treasury began bidding up the price of gold. In January 1934 the United States devalued the dollar by 41 percent, fixing the new "price" of pure gold at $35 an ounce and thus the new dollar at 13.71 grains of pure gold.

Henceforth the United States agreed to redeem its liabilities in gold only to foreign central banks or treasuries but not to American citizens or, indeed, individuals of any nation. This put the nation back on a weak form of gold standard, sometimes called a "qualified gold bullion standard." Under the definition cited earlier, it would hardly pass at all as a gold standard, but those who wanted to consider it as such emphasized that the dollar was the buying power of 13.71 grains of free gold on a free market for gold and such a market existed in London. For another two years there were better gold standards in the so-called Gold Bloc nations of France, Belgium, Switzerland, Holland, and Italy. One by one these left gold—Italy in 1934, Belgium in 1935, and the rest in 1936; France reduced her parity in three steps, 1936, 1937 and 1938, until it wound up with its 1928 relationship to the dollar. By now the American "qualified gold bullion standard," unworthy as it was by older criteria, was the best in the world. As the

French sometimes say, "In the land of the blind, the one-eyed man is king."

The 1933 devaluation of the dollar was unique in the annals of devaluation, and yet for the next generation many Americans were wont to generalize from it. We devalued then, we said, because prices had *fallen* too much. One may well ask what sort of a financial patent medicine a devaluation is that it cures all our economic ills. Most devaluations are reluctant, even forced, admissions by a nation that it has inflated its currency too much, or at least has done so to a greater degree than the nations around it. Devaluation is essentially a nation's way of declaring bankruptcy and trying to start over. Our 1971 and 1973 devaluations are of this kind. But a devaluation purposely to bring about a rise in prices and thereby cheat a segment of society in the course of doing so has always seemed to me to be particularly inexcusable.

Within a decade of the appearance of Gustav Cassel's and Joseph Kitchin's writings doubting that there was enough monetary gold, Professors Frank D. Graham and Charles Whittlesey of Princeton brought out *The Golden Avalanche*, which became a best seller. The so-called mint price of gold, the $35 an ounce figure of recent memory, was really not a market price at all, but rather the number of dollars, of 13.71 grains each, that a troy ounce of gold (480 grains) would coin into, i.e., almost exactly 35. So, when the United States cut the size of the dollar from the previous 23.22 grains to the new figure of 13.71 grains, it automatically changed the mint price from $20.67 to $35. This was a 69 percent rise in the price of gold, with the Mint required to "buy" (take as if to coin) all the gold anyone brought to it, without limit. The devaluation of January 1934 raised the dollar value of American reserves from $4 billion to $6.8 billion and stimulated the gold mining business beyond imagination. The stock of The Homestake Mining Company of California, the nation's largest gold mine, paid $2 *extra* monthly from July 1934 to May 1937 and in addition paid a special extra of $20 a share on December 5, 1935. The Treasury's holdings of gold grew from $6.8 billion in February 1934 to $22.7 billion in December 1941, at the time of the outbreak of World War II. There were growing fears of a gold inflation. Political unrest, too, was sending "hot money" to the United States from all over the world at this time.

At this stage most individuals with gold preferred to turn it into dollars, and that continued to be true for the next fifteen to twenty-five years. American holdings of gold reached their peak in September 1949 ($24.8 billion) and did not start flowing out, at least virtually without interruption, until early in 1958. Since then individuals have increasingly shown their preference for gold over dollars. It was a warning the United States should have acted upon more vigorously than it did at the time.

World War II, like World War I, produced some frightful inflations. As it drew to an end, the nations of the world again determined to set up a new world monetary system. Delegates from forty-four nations met at Bretton Woods, New Hampshire, in July 1944 and drew up a set of agreements providing for an International Monetary Fund, a sort of central bank of member central banks, into which they put deposits of gold, dollars, or their own currencies and from which they might borrow. The relationship of their monetary units to each other was to remain fixed, although within limits and by agreement it could be altered. The nations in the IMF elected to treat dollars as gold since dollars were redeemable to their treasuries and central banks on demand in gold. This made the dollar the "reserve currency" of the world. It created what economist Jacques Rueff calls another gold exchange standard situation, on a gigantic scale, with the U.S. Treasury and Federal Reserve playing much the same role that Montagu Norman's Bank of England did in the 1920s.

Meanwhile, a new goal had gained priority in the minds of the managers of our economy. The goal of stable prices had become passé. By the terms of the Full Employment Act of

1946, the President was instructed to seek to maintain full employment. It is not always easy to protect simultaneously the best interests of the laboring man and the best interests of businessmen. Anyway, it followed, in the minds of many economists, that a little inflation stimulated business activity and hence employment, whereas a raising of interest rates would cause unemployment. In fact, even stable prices were looked upon as really not satisfactory. So "a little inflation" was regarded favorably. Professor Paul Samuelson, whose economics principles textbook began to be a best seller in this era, said in his first edition that an annual inflation rate of 5 percent was quite acceptable and probably beneficial. The United States had had just that during 1939-1952, and it cost the dollar half its purchasing power in those thirteen years. In about 1960 a still newer priority came into vogue under President John Kennedy; this was economic growth, and a little inflation was said to stimulate that too. Inflation also made what growth there was seem greater than it actually was.

Of course, not everyone then, as now, was happy with the chronic deficits and the creeping inflation. There were periodic demands for greater economy in government, and a commission headed by ex-President Hoover reported on streamlining the executive branch of the government. A congressman from Nebraska, the late Howard Buffett, candidly pointed out what the American people had lost in 1933-1934 when the country abandoned the gold coin standard and instituted the qualified gold bullion standard in its stead, the latter forbidding American citizens to receive gold for their paper money. Congressman Buffett said that what chiefly influences a congressman's stand on any issue is his estimate of what most of his constituents want. That is where the election votes are and he wants to be reelected. Let me quote him. ". . . an economy-minded Congressman under our printing system is in the position of a fireman running into a burning building with a hose that is not connected with the water plug. His courage may be commendable, but he is not hooked up right at the other end of the line . . . with the tax payers to give him strength. When the people's right to restrain public spending by demanding gold coin was taken from them, the automatic flow of strength from the grass roots to enforce economy in Washington was disconnected." (*Commercial and Financial Chronical*, May 6, 1948).

As the United States over the ensuing two decades ran deficits year after year, with only rare exceptions, and increased its money supply in so doing, some of these surplus dollars found their way to European central banks. (They were presumably redeemable in gold, thus as good as gold.) In the 1940s they were very welcome and at times in the 1950s too, although by then their amount was causing anxieties. As major nations recovered from the ravages of war, they preferred to keep more of their reserves in gold itself, and some countries demanded gold for dollars. Despite our excess of merchandise exports over imports, which of itself would have attracted gold to the United States, this country had an adverse balance of payments. Short-term liabilities to foreigners rose from $6.9 billion in December 1945 to $13.6 in December 1957 to $28.8 in 1964 to $41.7 in December 1970 to $60.7 billion at the end of 1972. Obviously, our creditors became concerned as they watched us, year after year, live beyond our means, offer more and more IOUs, and draw down our most liquid assets, gold. American holdings of gold dropped from $22.9 billion in December 1957 to $15.5 billion in December 1964 to $11.1 in December 1970.

To reassure our creditors and make our own citizens aware of the worsening situation, our government applied a series of "band-aid" remedies, such as recalling families of servicemen abroad, forbidding American citizens to own gold abroad, taxing investments made overseas, lowering tourists' customs free allowances, to name just a few. When in 1960 the price of gold rose to over $40 on the free market for gold in London, we arranged with other central banks to dump enough gold onto that market to drive the price down to $35 again and remove the danger sign from public sight. That was in one sense the first appearance of the "two-tier system" of gold prices—$35 officially and something else on the London gold market. Eight years later, in March 1968, the hunger of gold buyers had become so insatiable that central bankers no longer wanted to dip into their reserves to hold down the price of gold. Total central bank gold reserves in the free world had actually shrunk because of this dipping, and did so despite free gold production of $11 billion of gold in that time. So now this coterie of central bankers, the United States a ringleader, proudly announced their solution, namely, have a two-tier system of pricing gold. They made a virtue, or at least a solution, of what they had regarded as a menace eight years before. Few experts thought this new-old solution would last long.

During those eight years, Treasury officials and others came forth with all kinds of promises and good resolves, but we never got around to the fundamental problem of balancing the budget and thus staunching the constant outflow of dollars and of restraining the buildup of short-term indebtedness. True, we had to wage a costly war in Asia in the 1960s, but if that was of top priority, then expenditures for other foreign aid, continuing farm price-support programs, and welfare programs should have been curtailed until we were in a position to afford them again. Instead we kept them all, created more dollars, some of which went abroad, and further increased our short-term liabilities. These traveling dollars enlarged the reserve accounts of foreign nations and encouraged them to inflate too—and they did. Since the American dollar was the world's reserve currency, an honor accorded the dollar and a special privilege accruing to the United States, we should have behaved more responsibly in maintaining its integrity.

Everyone knows the rest of the story, where all this has ended. With our trade situation worsening and short-term liabilities mounting at an alarming rate in the spring and summer of 1971, President Nixon finally announced on August

15 that we would no longer redeem our dollars in gold to central banks and treasuries. At the Smithsonian Institution in December we agreed to devalue the dollar by 7.9 percent. Many persons believed that was not enough, and the second 10-percent devaluation of February 12, 1973, plus the recent extreme weakness of the dollar, would appear to support that belief.

Some economists, and I am one of them, believe it is past time to consider returning to the gold standard, and preferably a gold coin standard to restore confidence in the American dollar. Some of our foreign friends have been hinting that a general devaluation of gold might be open for discussion.

The cry that there is not enough gold is becoming less and less plausible and it never was true. Gold revalued at, say, $87.50 an ounce would increase world monetary reserves two and a half times, or to $100 billion, and it would greatly stimulate gold mining, as it did in the 1930s. Moreover, the higher price would kill some of the industrial users' interest in gold—it already has the jewelers badly worried. If a gold standard restored confidence and provided more price stability, as one might hope it would, then hoarding gold would be less attractive, for gold pays no interest and is chiefly a defensive action against inflation. Much of the gold now hoarded would come out of hiding. In short, I believe there would no longer be a shortage of gold. Indeed, much of the present shortage is basically a consequence of inflation.

As for trying to substitute something else in the place of gold, which has repeatedly shown itself superior to eager rivals, that would involve a "selling" job to the world that would cost billions of dollars and make even Madison Avenue promoters shrink before the enormity of the undertaking. Why throw away a tradition, the world's respect for gold, that it has taken millennia to build up and is ours for the asking to use. Any attempt to replace it would be like deciding that we don't like our Great Lakes, one of God's great gifts to the United

States, and trying to remove them in order to put another water system of our own devising in their place.

A return to a gold standard might solve other problems too. Annual enactments of debt ceilings by Congress have become a farce, presidential impoundments of congressional appropriations are an annoyance, and congressional denials of responsibility for deficits are impossible to believe. So how do we discipline ourselves? Maybe we should restore the gold coin standard and put some of the control over our money back in the hands of the people, as suggested by Congressman Howard Buffett twenty-five years ago. Since Congress took that power away from the people in 1934, per capita federal expenditures have risen from about $115 to close to $2,500, and even in terms of dollars of a constant purchasing power there has been a *ten*-fold increase. This is a further reason for reconsidering the gold standard. It played a more important role in our economy, and our political system too, than many people realized.

7

Greenback Dollars And Federal Sovereignty 1861-1865

GARY NORTH

Economist, Chalcedon, Canoga Park, California

It was not that we declared paper a legal tender, but that we adopted a rule of action under the operation of which public credit was but an empty sound. It was not that the Treasury happened to be in a strait for money, but that it pretended to pay when it did not. The fact that the measure was accepted by the country as a just and proper one made the matter worse, because the sanction of public opinion was thus given to a ruinous principle, and the principle was, for this reason, more likely to become a standard policy.

Simon Newcomb (1865)

Inescapably, the most fundamental of all political questions is the question of sovereignty. Who has the authority to make the final decision in any particular situation (not simply brute power, but legitimacy—*authority*[1])? Which institution is the final court of appeal in the case of a dispute between men or institutions? In short, whose rule is legitimate in any given sphere of human existence?

There are many possible marks of sovereignty. It may be seen in a seal or a stamp; it may be designated by an instrument, such as the Roman magistrate's fasces or the scepter held by a bishop. Special clothing may characterize authority, such as black robes worn by judges, university graduates, or priests (all marks of sovereignty in the Middle Ages). But in the realm of economics the primary sign of sovereignty is the right to coin or print money. The political state for millennia has claimed exclusive monopoly rights in this area, to be shared with other agencies only by the state's explicit permission.

The implications of this right of coinage were understood far better in the ancient world, and especially the classical civilization of the Roman Empire, than today. Ethelbert Stauffer, theologian, numismatist, historian, has written that one of the earliest longings of mankind "is the longing for God to appear on earth."[2] The theological term for such a divine manifestation on earth is *theophany*. This longing for a theophany was a dominant theme of the politics of the ancient world, from Egypt and Babylon to Greece and Rome. "The official expression of this political philosophy," Stauffer writes, "is the classical coin. On the obverse of the coin we see the portrait of the ruler, decorated with the marks and emblems of deity, and framed in titles of divine dignity. For the ruler is the god who has become man. The reverse of the coin usually depicts the most symbolically potent event in the life of the ruler, his *advent*."[3] Significantly, the first to have the word *adventus* inscribed on the coins was Nero.[4] The coins had become political weapons, used first by Cleopatra and Augustus, since they were primary means of communication:

they were the newspaper, radio, and television of their day.[5]

To some extent, the modern world is returning to the theology and political philosophy of the ancient kingdoms. Men of today long for political salvation. The American sociologist Robert Nisbet has commented on this phenomenon: "To go to the root of a thing today is to go to its politics. Everything—business, science, race, the arts, even states of mind like hope and despair—must be placed in the category of politics. The word itself is talismanic. . . . What is business but the politics of production; education but the politics of teaching and research; religion but the politics of grace? Politics, in short, is not today what it was for the American intellectual for so many decades: a separate realm of values, a highly specialized and limited activity. It is a total process, unique perspective, even redemptive vision."[6] As the state becomes the primary agency of salvation—the absolute sovereign—as it was in the pagan ancient world, it arrogates unto itself the claim of total authority. But since this authority is illegitimate, the quest of the new statist theologians is now for total power.[7] Hayek's warning should be borne in mind: under such conditions, the worst members of society tend to get on top.[8]

Since the latter days of the American Civil War, it has been illegal for U.S. coins or paper money to bear the picture of any living American.[9] It is interesting that the 50 cent piece bearing the portrait of the late President John F. Kennedy (rushed into production in 1964, several years before the legal expiration date of the Franklin half dollars) has become a collectors' favorite. There is no numismatic reason for its great popularity; well over a billion of the coins had been minted by 1969. Professional numismatists shy away from investing in Kennedy halves.[10] Yet, the public throughout the world has made almost a fetish out of the coin. Even in 1971, when the paper dollar bill was not regarded by Europeans as a particularly impressive tip from an American tourist, the American could still delight a European with a copper-clad Kennedy half. The personal charisma of an otherwise mediocre President was transferred to the coins bearing his image. The modern world is not so far removed from ancient paganism.

The framers of the Constitution had gained considerable experience with the economic effects of an unlimited governmental sovereignty over the monetary unit. The paper money inflations of the colonial era, followed by the disastrous Revolutionary wartime inflation, and finally another threat of inflation by Daniel Shays' rebellious supporters in Massachusetts (1786-1787), served as sufficient warnings for the men in Philadelphia. Gerald Dunne has written that "the Founding Fathers regarded political control of monetary institutions with an abhorrence born of bitter experience, and they seriously considered writing a sharp limitation on such governmental activity into the Constitution itself. Yet they did not, and by 'speaking in silences' gave the government they founded the near-absolute authority over currency and coinage that has always been considered the necessary consequence of national sovereignty."[11] The results of their failure to include specific prohibitions against federal fiat money (as the Constitution does contain with regard to state governments) were not to become manifest until the great upheaval of 1861-1865. There had been preliminary warnings, however: the Panics of 1819, 1837, and 1857, all created by prior monetary inflations.

THE JACKSONIAN ERA

Andrew Jackson had been a "hard money" man from the very beginning of his political career. He had owned fairly extensive landholdings in Tennessee in the late 1790s, which he lost in the Panic of 1797. He had gone bankrupt in 1804. Never again was he to be anything resembling a high-flying speculator. During the Panic of 1819—this nation's first truly modern depression—he had reaffirmed his resolute opposition to fractional reserve banking at any level, state or national. He was convinced, as he wrote in a letter to William B. Lewis, that banking involving note issue of any kind was unconstitutional.[12] Jackson was never to waver from this belief. He was to repeat himself on this point to Thomas Hart Benton during the years of the struggle against the Second Bank of the United States.[13] As Rothbard notes, many of the anti-bank, hard money leaders in Jackson's Democratic party, including Benton and James K. Polk, first came to this outlook during the Panic of 1819.[14]

It was well understood by most political leaders at the national level in the 1830s and 1840s that only gold and silver coins could serve as legal tender payments for all debts. Daniel Webster, a strong supporter of the Bank of the United States, a believer in "conservative" fractional reserve banking so long as it maintained full redeemability in coin, and an opponent of Jackson, was forced to admit that "if we understand by currency the *legal money* of the country, and that which constitutes a lawful tender for debts, and is the statute measure of value, then, undoubtedly, nothing is included but gold and silver. Most unquestionably there is no legal tender, and there can be no legal tender, in this country, under the authority of this government or any other, but gold and silver, either the coinage of our own mints, or foreign coins, at rates regulated by Congress. This is a constitutional principle, perfectly plain, and of the very highest importance."[15] Indeed, it was of crucial importance, and the abandonment of this fundamental constitutional principle was to lead to the great monetary disruptions, North and South, after 1861.

American political parties, then as now, were not rigidly doctrinal and could encompass men of fairly wide persuasions on any given issue, but the Jacksonians were generally suspicious of banking, if not utterly hostile. William Gouge, one of the intellectual leaders in the Jacksonian camp, wrote a book which was to become a kind of touchstone, *A Short History of Paper Money and Banking in the United States* (1833). Gouge saw the close interdependence between the monopoly privileges of currency creation held by the banks and the need of governments for cheap loans. He was convinced that banks were not so much a conspiracy foisted upon unsuspecting legislators as the express creations of the legislatures. His opposition to fractional reserve banking was based entirely on principle; personalities were completely irrelevant.

> As banks are the creatures of Government, all the evils they produce must be ascribed to the Government. It is to afford opportunities for speculation to themselves, their personal friends and their political partisans, that our law-givers establish Banks. It was through the attempt to carry on the war [of 1812] by means of Bank notes and Bank credits, that the suspension of specie payments was produced. It was through the connivance of the Government, that the suspension of specie payments was so long continued. It was through the issue of treasury notes, that the amount of Bank notes in circulation was immediately increased. . . . It is of very little moment whether it is Mr. WIGGINS or Mr. SPRIGGINS that is president of a Bank, or whether the JONES' or the GILES' are directors. *The fault is in the system.* Give the management of it to the wisest and best men in the country, and still it will produce evil.[16]

In his war against the Second Bank of the United States, Jackson decided to transfer the government's funds to the state banks, thus removing a substantial portion of the Bank's reserves. This decision later drew the criticism of hard money proponents like Benton. "Old Bullion" himself announced in 1837: "I did not join in putting down the Bank of the United States to put up a wilderness of local banks. I did not join in putting down the currency of a national bank, to put up a national paper currency of a thousand local banks."[17] From Jackson's day until quite recently, the President's decision to transfer the government's funds to state banks has been regarded as ultimately inflationary. The implication is, of course, that the Bank, as the nation's central bank, was more conservative, more responsible than unregulated (or less regulated) state banks. Only recently has this thesis been challenged. Hugh Rockoff has estimated that the transfer may have increased the money supply by less than 2 percent.[18] State banks were far more inflationary as depositories than the Independent Treasury system, introduced in 1840, abandoned in 1841, and reintroduced in 1846. That system was not involved in fractional reserves. But state banks may have been no worse than the Second Bank. Thus, the estimate of Roger Taney—Secretary of the Treasury in 1833 and later Chief Justice of the Supreme Court—was probably correct. His justification for the use of state banks in preference to a central bank for the government's deposits was based on the question of limited versus total sovereignty: "For no one of these corporations will possess that absolute, and almost unlimited dominion over the property of the citizens of the United States, which the present bank holds, and which enables it at any moment, at its own pleasure, to bring distress upon any portion of the community, whenever it may deem it useful to its interest to make its power felt. The influence of each of the state banks is necessarily limited to its own immediate neighborhood, and they will be kept in check by the other local banks."[19] If the people must tolerate the sovereignty of banks in currency matters, let that sovereignty be limited and local. The Jacksonian persuasion was decentralist to the core.

There was another factor in the Jacksonians' hostility to banking. Bray Hammond, the leading historian of banking during the Jacksonian period (and an uncompromising admirer of central banking), has called attention to this factor. What most offended them about banking was the character of the banks as limited liability corporations. Unincorporated partnerships in which the partners bore the full personal responsibility for the failure of the bank were not regarded with the same intense hatred.[20] Grant a bank a corporate charter, however, and a "vast monopoly," to use Taney's words, is created.[21] As Benton said on the floor of the Senate, "This exclusive privilege is contrary to the genius of our Government, which is a government of equal rights and not of exclusive privileges. . . ."[22] In his massive book, *Thirty Years' View* (1854), Benton listed as one of several basic flaws in fractional reserve banking the fact of "the exemption of the stockholders from individual responsibility in the failure of the bank." He argued that "This privilege derogates from the common law, is contrary to the principle of partnerships, and injurious to the rights of the community."[23] Here is the essence of the Jacksonian persuasion: anti-monopoly, anti-special privilege, and very much pro-personal responsibility.

There is no question concerning the basic thrust of Jacksonian economic theory and policy: at the national level, Adam Smith had triumphed. No other period in American history could more reasonably be described as laissez-faire.[24] Modern historians are for the most part repelled by this fact; they try to find signs here and there that the government really was quite active in economic affairs. At the state government level, this was true: railroads, canals, schools, and other basic institutions were financed in part by tax revenues. But at the federal level, the evidence is clear. A few post roads, a bit of surveying here and there, federal deposits in state banks (which the Independent Treasury system was drawn up to limit): such was the extent of the "positive intervention" of the federal government.[25] Reading contemporary historians as they seek to evaluate the economic thought of the Jackson era, one can sense the feelings of horror in the hearts of our modern, "neutral" scholars. Bray Hammond writes: "Jackson sought first to keep the federal government 'pure' and modestly within its constitutional limits—its virtue to be not that it did great things but that it left its people free to do them. He succeeded too well."[26] But Glyndon Van Deusen's comments are the most forthright; in his *obiter dicta* we see the operating presuppositions of the vast bulk of modern historical scholarship: "It [Jacksonianism] was also, in the opinion of this writer, a movement so heavily imbued with archaic notions about corporations, currency, banking and do-nothing national government, that it would sooner or later have gone down to political defeat, even without the aid of the great depression [of 1837] which it helped to bring on."[27] Jeffersonian agrarianism—the philosophy of limited government and the strict construction of the Constitution—"lay like a heavy hand upon their [Jacksonian Democrats'] shoulders."[28] And finally, so that his readers might not miss his "subtle" earlier remarks, he writes: "At the same time, their narrow view of the function of the national government repeatedly kept them from using the government for constructive ends. . . . Their hard money ideas were negative and inadequate for dealing with the problem at hand—how to establish a currency and credit that would be both sound and ample."[29] A currency both sound and ample; with enough of it, but not too much of it; money to grow on but not enough to choke on; eating our cake but having it, too: here is the rhetoric of the modern inflationist, always searching for the impossible, and then, when the balance proves impossible in practice, siding with those favoring monetary expansion. Always willing to inflate the currency to stimulate growth, then hesitating when the artificially stimulated boom turns into a bust when the monetary expansion slows or stops, and then returning to more expansion to bring back the boom: here is the macroeconomics of contemporary scholarship. It is not surprising that modern scholars are appalled by the Age of Jackson, an era in which a President of the United States could announce: "We have no emergencies that make banks necessary to aid the wants of the treasury; we have no load of national debt to provide for, and we have on actual deposit a large surplus."[30]

The American Civil War was to destroy the appeal of the Jacksonian philosophy, even as the depression of the 1930s destroyed the "conservative" interventionism of the post-Civil War period. Professor Sidney Fine echoes the opinion of most of his academic colleagues when he writes: "Thus in 1865, though Americans saw a new industrial society emerging, they were without an adequate philosophy of state action to cope with the problems of society. What was needed," we are informed by Professor Fine, "was a new philosophy of the state, a new liberalism embodying something of the spirit of Jeffersonianism but ready to use government as an agency to promote the general welfare. Industrial America made necessary the evolution of the general-welfare state."[31]

There had been state economic intervention prior to the Civil War (although little federal intervention). As Professor Goodrich has concluded, such activity for "internal improvements" was in large measure a frontier phenomenon, "a great instance of frontier collectivism." As the communities grew, private business tended to replace the formerly statist activities.[32] Furthermore, as Fine himself notes, the range of economic activities in which the federal government was involved shrank noticeably just prior to the Civil War.[33] State bonds and securities, so popular with London and other foreign investors in the 1820s and 1830s, lost that popularity abroad in the 1840s as a result of outright forfeiture by several state legislatures.[34] There was widespread resentment by voters against taxation and a willingness to abandon investors to their fate, especially foreign investors. Thus, it should not be surprising to learn that states were compelled to reduce the extent of their financial aid for projects of economic development.

The question then that remains is one concerning the impact of the Civil War on American attitudes toward government enterprise. The democratic strain in Jacksonian thought, so favored by contemporary historians, was to further "a new philosophy of the state" after 1865. Yet it was not the war itself which created industrialism, that industrialism which Fine and most other recent scholars believe made necessary an expansion of federal economic intervention. The war may not have retarded industrialization, as Thomas Cochran has argued, but few scholars are willing to assert that it intensified the industrialization process already well developed in the 1850s.[35] What brought the new philosophy of state action into being was an acceptance of the legitimacy of federal centralization in all spheres of economic and political life. It was therefore a shift in opinion concerning the legitimate use of federal power, or, in Nisbet's framework, the shift from federal power to federal authority. When the phrase (pre-1860) "the United States are" became "the United States is" (post-1865), something more than a mere alteration of grammar was involved. What was involved was a revolution in the concept of federal sovereignty, that most crucial of political questions.

THE CIVIL WAR

"The problems of Reconstruction finance were sewn in the thirteen feverish months following Lincoln's election," writes Irwin Unger. "The acute political crisis, the unprecedented drain on the country's human and economic resources, the releasing of restraints as the political and military shock jarred men loose from customary practices—all combined to raise up a host of new financial problems that would trouble America for a generation."[36] The most important of these Reconstruction economic issues was the money question. Professor Nugent says that "No one realized it in 1865, but money was destined to become the chief perennial issue in national politics for over thirty years, reaching a culmination in the election of 1896 with William Jennings Bryan's campaign for free silver."[37] The year 1862 saw the coming of the greenbacks, and both in symbol and its implications for federal power, there is hardly a more important event in American economic history.

Any statistical estimate of the actual costs of the Civil War is bound to be faulty. Too many human costs are simply not subject to statistical calculation. How much is lost, for example, by the death of some potential inventor or financier or clergyman (or potential father of the same) on some long-forgotten battlefield? What might have been accomplished for human betterment with capital otherwise expended in four years of carnage? We can barely guess, constructing some hypothetical "as if" historical framework as a model. Another more concrete limitation on assessing the costs of the war is the woefully incomplete status of economic statistics prior to the 1870s. The records we do have are very often confused, misleading, or unusable for the purposes at hand. Monetary statistics prior to 1867 are incomplete. In fact, the statistics concerning banking are better for the years prior to 1863 than after, ironically because the framers of the National Banking Act of 1863 were so overconfident about the new plan's potential for integrating all of the nation's banks that organized federal collecting of state bank statistics ceased.[38]

We do know a few facts, however. In 1860, the national debt was in the range of $65 million. By 1865 the figure had skyrocketed to a staggering $2.8 billion.[39] In 1860, the federal government had annual expenditures of about $63 million. In 1865 the expenditures totaled almost $1.3 billion for the year.[40] Financing such unprecedented costs involved the Union in a fiscal revolution.

Four-fifths of the expenditures of the federal government during the war were paid for through borrowing and the creation of fiat paper money.[41] Much of the borrowed money itself was the creation of the banking system. The money and banking statistics, however flawed, do testify to a vast expansion of money during the Civil War in the North. (Oddly enough, the South's well-known experience with paper money and the resulting price inflation—"Save your Confederate money, boys, the south shall rise again"—has received only a fraction of the scholarly attention focused on the North's experience.[42] The incredible array of money and quasi-moneys also testifies to the difficulty of assessing either the monetary policies of the era or the extent of the monetary inflation.

First, there was specie: silver coins (which had been driven out of circulation before 1861 by Gresham's Law, since the legal exchange rate, fixed by federal law, between gold and silver had artificially overvalued the silver, as California and Australian gold discoveries had made gold more plentiful), gold coins, and subsidiary token coins. By early 1862, the gold coins were no longer in circulation. Gold was used to purchase foreign exchange and to pay tariffs on imported goods (and to pay the interest on government bonds), but it commanded a varying premium over paper money throughout the war. Second, bank notes of the state banks. Third, bank deposits, although contemporaries generally did not understand that these constituted money as such. Fourth, after 1861, non-interest bearing legal tender notes (old demand notes and the U.S. notes, i.e., greenbacks). Fifth, after 1861, certificates of indebtedness. Sixth, after 1862, postage currency. Seventh, after 1863, fractional currency ("shinplasters," of paper money with a face value of less than $1). Eighth, after 1863, various interest-bearing, legal tender notes. Finally, the coin, bullion, and paper money in the Treasury.[43] This has led the major historian of the greenbacks, Wesley Clair Mitchell, to comment: "It is altogether impossible to determine whether there was a close correspondence between the course of prices and the volume of the currency, as was affirmed by some writers and denied by others, because, as it has been shown at length, the quantity of money in use cannot be ascertained."[44]

Using the extended definition of the money supply supplied by Mitchell (but the more recent figures supplied by *Historical Statistics of the United States* in those cases where Mitchell's figures have been updated), we find that in 1865 there was about $1.7 billion in various currencies or near-currencies (not counting gold coin), and $689 million in bank deposits, for a total of $2.4 billion. In 1860, specie totaled $207 million, bank deposits were also at the $207 million level, and deposits were about $310 million, for a total of about $750 million. In addition, according to William Donlon, a specialist in paper money numismatics, Civil War counterfeiting was "unusually prevalent," and it accounted for one-third of the currency in circulation.[45] This, of course, is only a rough estimate, but it is interesting that the subject of counterfeiting and its impact on the aggregate money supply is virtually unexplored in the professional economists' studies of the Civil War. If he is correct, the total money supply may have reached $3 billion, or about the same level as the national debt stood in 1865.

This total is probably too high. The tables in *Historical Statistics* do not include the various debt certificates as money, but merely list "other U.S. currency." These figures produce a total of $1.6 billion, considerably less than Mitchell's total, but still over twice the money supply of 1860, even if we ignore the counterfeiting factor. Thus, between two and four times as much money was in circulation in 1865 as had been present in 1860.

Milton Friedman does not attempt to estimate the money supply in 1865, but he writes that the money supply in 1867 was probably lower than it had been at the end of the war. He estimates that the 1867 figure was $1.59 billion.[46] The price level had declined, Friedman asserts, by 25 percent in the intervening two years.[47] Thus, it would seem safe to estimate that the total money supply, including counterfeit currency, was in the $2 billion range, and possibly higher. In an earlier study, Friedman presented conclusions concerning his estimates of such matters as the velocity of money and aggregate price changes in the Civil War, World War I, and World War II.[48] For what such exercises are worth—and if taken too seriously, they are probably more trouble than they are worth[49]—he estimates that the aggregate price level increased between the outbreak of hostilities and the high price point of the war (January 1865) by a factor of 2.3.[50] This figure compares with Mitchell's estimate of a doubling in price of two-thirds of all commodities in the same period.[51] Wages, Mitchell argues, did not keep pace with prices.

Aggregate figures of prices and wages conceal a great deal.

Which groups benefited and which ones paid more than their share of the war's costs? On this point, obviously a crucial one, historians cannot seem to agree.

Farmers: These were the most numerous segment of the population throughout the nineteenth century. Mitchell concludes that farmers as a group were net losers during the war, "among the most unfortunate" of all producers.[52] But Emerson Fite explicitly rejects Mitchell's conclusion in the case of western farmers; they prospered, paid off mortgages and other debts, saw their incomes grow, and the West received eager immigrants from eastern farming areas. This would indicate a fall in productivity of eastern farms, however. Depopulation of eastern rural areas was widespread.[53] The effects of price inflation and war expenditures did not hit all farmers equally.

Wage-earners: Mitchell states unequivocally that "in no case did the wage-earners escape a considerable loss of real income. . . . While the fluctuations of real wages are seen to have been by no means uniform in all cases, there is no industry in which the advance in money wages kept pace with the advance in prices."[54] Most workers—98 percent of them—earned less than $2.50 per day in 1860, and they did not all work throughout the year, given seasonal employment and trade cycle disruptions.[55] Most men earned from $1 to $1.50 per day. Money wages for the highest paid workers in 1860 appreciated least rapidly—by one-fourth to one-third—while lower paid workers received increases of two-thirds to three-fourths.[56] Real wages fell, given the doubling of prices.[57] In a later study, Mitchell admits the weakness of the available data; nevertheless, he remains convinced that wage-earners were worse off in 1865 than in 1860.[58] Currency depreciation, he estimates, amounted to "a confiscation of perhaps a fifth or sixth of real incomes."[59] (The costs were borne willingly, for the most part, except in 1864, when the gold premium was at its highest.[60]) Thus, concludes Mitchell, "the chief cause of the extraordinary advance in American prices between 1862 and 1865 was the substitution of irredeemable paper for specie as the money in which prices were quoted."[61]

Michell's claim that greenbacks and other fiat currency caused the fall in real wages has been challenged by Alchian and Kessel. They have argued, rather, that the wages of laborers fell because of factors other than monetary depreciation. They concentrate on three of these factors: the boom conditions in 1860, distorting Mitchell's base-year figures (least important); the rise in the rate of foreign exchange relative to domestic price increases (due to unfavorable terms of trade when the South's cotton exports disappeared); and the tax system used to finance the war. They go so far as to argue that monetary inflation may have kept wages higher than they would have been if the North had raised tax revenues by means of additional tariff and excise tax increases.[62] Mitchell, while admitting that war tariffs and internal taxes "also are responsible for some portion of the advance in prices,"[63] still insists that "the suspension of specie payments and the legal-tender acts must be held responsible for all of the far-reaching economic disturbances following from the price upheaval."[64] Alchian and Kessel have made this dogmatic statement untenable.

But why should monetary inflation be seen as a potentially defensible form of taxation? The central difficulty with the "tax on cash balances" involved in all monetary expansion is its unpredictability. No one is quite sure exactly who will bear the brunt of the tax burden. No one is even very clear in retrospect, as the conflicting interpretations of economic historians should indicate. It leads to a misallocation of scarce economic resources because of the illusion fostered by higher money wages and higher paper profits. It creates a boom-bust cycle through its interference in the rate of interest.[65] It penalizes the less informed, less mobile members of the community, since professional speculators (including those economists who understand economics—more numerous, proportionately, in the 1850s than today) are better able to hedge against and even profit from changes in relative prices. Monetary inflation makes it far more difficult for citizens to assess the true burdens of government expenditures. Furthermore, it makes it far easier for government officials to blame the "evil speculators" for the economic difficulties. This last criticism is no idle charge; in the North and the South, such arguments were freely indulged in.[66]

There is an ironic note to the search for those who bore the heaviest tax burden as a result of currency depreciation. Clerks employed in the federal government's service were clearly heavy losers.[67] Senator Sherman, in his speech in favor of the National Banking Act in 1863, alluded to this fact in his criticism of U.S. notes (for which he had voted regularly).[68] Draftees into the army were also hard-pressed, although volunteers did fare better because of the high bounties paid to volunteers.[69]

Holders of government paper money and bonds saw their assets decline in value.[70] Obviously, as in all inflations, those on fixed incomes suffered. In fact, the faithful bore the brunt of the costs. Simon Newcomb, in a superb little book published in 1865 prior to the end of the war, explained it as well as anyone ever has: "A system of paper money may be described, in general, as *a convenient device for throwing the entire burden of an extraordinary expense upon that class of the community who have the most faith in paper money.*"[71] He went on to cite the inflation of the American Revolution. The Tories immediately spent the paper, leaving the patriots to watch it depreciate. Those who believe neither in the cause nor the means employed to achieve victory escape the burdens. This is inevitably the case in any war financed through monetary inflation, which means all of them. The cynics come out the economic victors.

Beyond the question of relative tax burdens, relative prices, gold premium, and foreign exchange is the overriding question of political sovereignty. The Civil War left a legacy of confusion in the monetary and fiscal spheres, including the boom-bust cycles of the next generation. But when we reflect on the fact that the national debt of $2.5 billion was reduced to $1.5 billion by 1885, and in 1916 it was down to $1.25 billion (which World War I was to escalate permanently), we begin to understand that the dollars and cents problem was less fundamental than the revolution in the concept of federal sovereignty. Bray Hammond has grasped this fact better than any other recent historian (he rejoices in the fact of that revolution), and his book, *Sovereignty and an Empty Purse*, is well named. The debates that took place in Congress in 1861 and 1862 concerning war finance and the legal tender question reveal that the participants understood quite well what they were arguing. Would the Jacksonian-Jeffersonian tradition of strict construction, limited government, and fiscal frugality be abandoned? *The New York Times*, following the lead of most other newspapers in the North, swung over to the fiat money side in early 1862. It editorialized (January 6, 1862): all persons "who regard the government as anything more than a confederation of states to be broken or weakened at will by secession or rebellion—all who believe the federal authority a power for the general good of the whole people as well as the symbol of sovereignty and allegiance—will welcome this resumption of one of its most important rights and duties."[72] What was being "resumed" was the inflationist tradition of the Revolutionary War; what was not being resumed was the payment of gold for paper money. (Banks had suspended payment in late December 1861, the week before the editorial appeared.)

George Pendleton, a congressman from Ohio, stood before his colleagues on January 29, 1862, and delivered perhaps the most cogent speech against legal tender fiat currency in U.S. history. (Yet even he was to be swept into the greenback camp before the war had ended, so strong was the inflationary opinion of his day.) Legal tender, he said, is a violation of contract, a departure from the philosophy of the Founding

Fathers, unconstitutional, and an illegitimate extension of the federal power.

> In all its external relations, standing among the nations of the earth, the Government of the United States is sovereign, and is invested with all the attributes of sovereignty; but in its relations to its own citizens, in its relations to the States, in its relations to its own constituents, it has no power except that which is granted. It has no original power; its powers are all delegated, and delegated by the terms of the Constitution itself. I repudiate the idea that all the sovereign power which rightfully resides in the nation must necessarily find expression in any department of the Government, whether it be national or State.[73]

It was a strong speech, and it went unheeded, even by Pendleton in later years.

As is the case in most crucial political questions, the appeal to practical considerations—pragmatism—won out. Clement Vallandigham, the continual Democratic thorn in Republican sides, appealed to the Constitution, but devoted most of his efforts to showing why the taxation of fiat money was not necessary. The nation was wealthy, and the govenment had the power to lay taxes. He well understood that his colleagues, like most politicians, desperately desired to hide the true costs of their schemes from their constituents. Unwilling to use direct taxes, they were "willing and eager to use force upon the people instead of taxes, the unconstitutional, despotic, and most disastrous coercion of a paper currency to be received in satisfaction of every debt. . . . If you are afraid of the people, be afraid to do wrong, not to do right."[74] But he was outvoted. John Crisfield of Maryland argued that there was not enough time to tax, and "we are left with no option. The supply of precious metals is inadequate for our wants."[75] Here is the age-old argument for monetary inflation, as popular with

Keynesians, Technocrats, Social Crediters, and Chicago School economists (when they are not doffing a theoretical cap to 100-percent reserve banking and slowly falling prices, just before they return to their call for 3-percent to 5-percent continuous monetary expansion) in the twentieth century as it was then. There is just not enough money to go around, *given the level of present prices* and the present distribution of resources.[76] Apparently, what governments need during wars is lots of green paper slips; resources will take care of themselves.[77] As Newcomb put it, "if we need twice as much cloth for uniforms, all we need is to reduce the official definition of one yard and we will have twice as many yards of cloth. Admittedly, our soldiers would be twice as tall, and therefore still short of uniforms, but think of the fear such giants will induce in the enemy!"[78]

But would the currency not depreciate? No, answered Crisfield, and endless other defenders of the greenbacks, since they will be convertible into 6-percent bonds. But the bonds will not sell at par. Not so; they will be easily sold for greenbacks, since the greenbacks will be plentiful.[79] Again, citing Newcomb, we can keep two ships from drifting in a storm by lashing them to each other.[80] Yet both in the North and the South, legislators argued some variation on this line of reasoning.[81] So the value of the currency fell, and the bonds fell as well, unless, as in the North, certain issues bore interest payments in gold. Of course, if the gold was worth twice as much as a comparable face amount of currency, then the actual rate of interest paid was double this official 6 percent. But somehow the credit of the government would be saved, for the bonds would stay at par. Newcomb said it best: "Government credit is a fact, not a mathematical theorem. It is not to be measured by calculating our resources, praising our honesty, and demonstrating our ability to pay, but by observing what our bonds sell for in the public market."[82] Few legislators, North or South, wanted that kind of a test. It was easier to give speeches.

What of constitutional restraints? We have only one Constitution, announced Thaddeus Stevens: self-preservation.[83] He feared the effects of legal tender, but he promised that only $150 million would be necessary.[84] Yet he voted for $300 million more within the next thirteen months.

Senator Timothy Howe used an approach which had been used effectively by men like Daniel Webster in their earlier battles against Jacksonian economic stringency. He argued that all of the practices which the hard money men were denouncing as unconstitutional and ultimately disastrous were already fully accepted features of the American economy. U. S. notes will be irredeemable. Why should that make any difference? All paper money is ultimately irredeemable, whether issued by private banks or governments. There is never enough specie available to meet the calls for redemption if everyone should want his specie at one point in time. Howe delivered an extremely telling speech against fractional reserves and the fraud involved in promising men that their paper claims on gold or silver are to be honored, but only if they are not actually brought in for redemption.[85] Yet, instead of concluding that anything less than 100 percent specie reserves would not be permitted, he only asked why the banks rather than the federal government should have this right of creating fiat money. He also refused to consider the possibility that the threat of specie withdrawals does act as a restraining factor on bank note issues, whereas with a pure fiat standard such a direct restraint does not exist. Since the government could never redeem all the notes at once anyway, it should not promise to pay any specie at all. He then offered the classic argument of all greenbackers, well over a century old in this country, and growing in popularity even today within supposedly "conservative" circles: "Make the notes like the coin, a sufficient tender for all debts due to both the Government and to individuals. Congress has the power to 'regulate the value' of both. *Let the value of both be the same.*"[86] Like the kings of old, wrote Newcomb, our rulers dislike the laws of the market, laws that permit the prices of commodities desired by them to rise under the pressures of increased demand. The leader "attributes all this to the machinations of his enemies, and the heartless selfishness of individuals, and forthwith resorts to penal and mandatory legislation for a remedy. He enacts that his promises to pay shall be as valuable as gold. Gold instantly disappears. He then enacts that they shall be legal tender. Immediately every man who has goods for sale doubles or trebles their prices, so that the government is still no better off than before."[87]

With the suspension of specie payments by the New York banks on Monday, December 31, 1861, $100 worth of paper currency would no longer purchase what had been $100 worth of gold the week before. The gold premium, which was really a premium on foreign exchange, never disappeared during the war. From the end of 1861 until the resumption of specie payments in 1879, the United States was in effect on a floating exchange rate system with respect to foreign currencies, the price of gold serving as the equivalent of the price of all foreign currencies that maintained convertibility into gold (primarily England, as far as American trade was concerned, but also Germany and France).[88] When, in July 1864, the gold premium climbed to $285 in greenbacks for $100 in gold (or $35 in gold for $100 in greenbacks)—the high point in the premium during the greenback era—there could be little question that Senator Howe's hypothesis was incorrect: Congress (or kings) cannot regulate the value of money. The market performs that service; no other agency can.

Senator John Sherman of Ohio, whose name was attached to some of the most unsound pieces of federal economic legislation in the nineteenth century, announced, quite accurately, that the bankers wanted Congress to pass the greenback legislation.[89] Let us bow, he said, to their expert opinion. Almost a year later, to the day, Sherman spoke in favor of another piece of legislation, the National Banking Act, and criticized the greenbacks for their use by the banks as legal reserves for new rounds of inflationary bank note expansion.[90] Without gold to support their notes, the New York banks were officially breaking New York state banking law; they needed something that was legal tender to back up their note issue. As Hammond has noted, "Instead of being curbed (as some people supposed later), the powers of the banks were augmented by the legal tender issues."[91] But in 1862, Sherman was four-square behind the legal tender fiat paper money. We have no choice, he argued; we have debts to pay, supplies to buy. Let us waive our constitutional doubts and proceed.[92] What does it matter that this legal tender status of government fiat money in some way may violate contracts? We do it all the time!

> But Congress every day passes laws that affect the value of property and of money, and therefore incidentally the value of contracts. The other day the Senator from Iowa [Mr. Grimes] introduced a bill to establish a street railroad in the city of Washington. We were all in favor of it; but did any Senator dream that by doing that he was impairing the obligation of contracts? And yet we affected the value of omnibuses that now run on the streets of Washington. Every act that you pass, almost every event in our political history now, impairs the value of property.[93]

So why be squeamish now? Most of them weren't, as it turned out a few weeks later.

But economics played only a partial role in Sherman's thought. The hard facts of economics were not his ultimate concern. His ultimate concern was federal sovereignty. A year later he spoke:

> But, sir, there is still a higher motive for the passage of this bill. It will promote a sentiment of nationality. There can be no doubt of it. The policy of this country ought to be to make everything national as far as possible; to

nationalize our country, so that we shall love our country. If we are dependent on the United States for a currency and a medium of exchange, we shall have a broader and more generous nationality. The want of such nationality, I believe, is one of the great evils of the times. This doctrine of State rights, which substitutes a local community—for, after all, the most powerful State is but a local community—instead of the United States of America, has been the evil of our times; and it is that principle of State rights, that bad sentiment that has elevated State authority above the great national authority, that has been the main instrument by which our Government is sought to be overthrown.[94]

This time, however, he was not arguing in favor merely of fiat money; this time he was supporting the creation of a national banking system. He took Hamilton's old idea that a national bank would unify the nation's sentiment through shared debt, and converted it into the doctrine that a national banking currency would unify the nation's loyalty. As Hammond writes, "It was a time when most men committed to uncompromising defense of the Union—whether in Congress or not—began committing themselves to a militant elevation of all federal powers, long neglected, and to a curtailment of states' powers."[95]

Many of those who had originally opposed the idea of paper money, both in the North and South, were impelled by the crisis and a new ideology to reverse their older views. Secretary of the Treasury Chase, an opponent of fiat currency in 1861 and after the war when he served as Chief Justice of the Supreme Court, defended the greenbacks in 1862. Senator Pendleton, the eloquent opponent of greenbacks, eventually became a strong supporter of the idea. The economic boom created by the fiat money made friends out of former enemies, especially western farmers. The citizenry's allegiance to hard money Jacksonian principles shifted radically during the war.

The precedent, as Newcomb warned in 1865, was not easily broken.[96]

The real question was the question of federal sovereignty. The economic records of the period may be poor and incomplete, and the interpretations of the historians may differ as to which of the wartime policies caused what economic results. There may be little assurance as to which groups paid more or less of the costs of the war. Nevertheless, the passage of the first legal tender act on February 25, 1862, marks a major transition in U.S. history. While $450 million worth of greenbacks were authorized during the next thirteen months, and probably $431 million were actually distributed, it was that first issue of $150 million that was crucial—crucial as a political precedent, not as an economic factor of major impact. Hammond, in a lengthy paragraph, has spelled out the implications of that decision better than anyone has:

> Though somewhat limited in scope and temporary in purpose, the act was revolutionary. It went counter to the principle of the tenth amendment that the federal government possessed only those powers specifically assigned to it by the Constitution. It was contrary to the understanding that the authors of the Constitution had intended the power of issuing paper money be withheld from the federal government as well as forbidden the states. It was contrary to the popular belief, religious as well as economic, that there could be no money, real and legal, but silver and gold and that the Almighty, as professed three years later by a Secretary of the Treasury, Hugh McCulloch, had placed the precious metals in the earth for the specific purpose of providing mankind with a standard of value and medium of exchange. It was contrary to the monetary practice of the United States since its formation—a practice the government had never before departed from. It recovered from desuetude the responsibility of the federal sovereignty to do what had

hitherto been generally considered both unconstitutional and inexpedient. It established a national monetary medium which derived its value from the will of the government. It overrode state laws.[97]

The messianic sovereignty of federal power was announced more openly on February 25, 1862, than ever before. The government had accomplished the impossible—on paper, at least. It had turned stones into bread.[98] It had created wealth merely by stamping ink on little green slips of paper. It announced, on principle, not the advent of a golden age, but the advent of a verdant age, "as good as gold." If we are to search for the intellectual roots of the New Deal, we should not look to the "Age of Jackson," as Schlesinger has tried to convince us; we should look at that legislation which marked the end of the Age of Jackson.

POSTSCRIPT: THE MYTH OF "LINCOLN MONEY"

The old Jacksonian fervor against the monopolists, the bankers, the "moneyed interests," was transformed from a hard money position to a pro-greenback position during the Civil War. The populists of the late nineteenth century were the spiritual, though not the intellectual, heirs of the more nativist strain of the Jacksonian movement.[99]

The neo-populist economics of the twentieth century, including the foreign import of Social Credit (which achieved political success not in England but in western Canada), represents a throwback to the greenbackers of the 1860s and 1870s. Today, however, this fiat money philosophy dominates the American right wing's more radical fringes. The poorly printed and widely read books from the Omni Press of Hawthorne, California, continue the tradition.

One of the most popular of these peculiar books is Gertrude Coogan's *Money Creators*, first published in 1935.[100] It had gone through nine printings by 1963, but none between 1943 and 1963. The opening paragraph of the first chapter is illuminating: "When Lincoln wanted to issue constitutional money, he was violently opposed by the 'Bullion Brokers,' as the international bankers were called in those days. Lincoln was, perhaps, the greatest exponent of honesty and of the Constitution that this country has had since Washington. He persisted in demanding honest money, until he was silenced." I have searched this paragraph diligently, and I have yet to find a single sentence that is true.

First of all, Lincoln had begun his political career as a Whig. The Whigs were opponents of the more conservative Jacksonians (using "conservative" to mean limited government, hard money ideas). In the 1830s, Lincoln had explicitly opposed Jackson's hard money policies. In 1839 he delivered a speech in Springfield, Illinois, attacking President Van Buren's proposal of an Independent Treasury (nonfractional reserve) system, and he actually defended Biddle's Second Bank of the United States. [101]

Second, there is little evidence to indicate that Lincoln was a prime mover in the greenback legislation of 1862. (I am being cautious; I have found absolutely no evidence of his direct intervention one way or the other.) His Secretary of the Treasury, Salmon P. Chase, initially opposed the legislation, although after the suspension of specie payments by the banks he reluctantly capitulated. [102] His hope, as he stated in the Annual Treasury Report of 1862, was to resume specie payments. [103] The real leader—the "Father of the Greenbacks," as Mitchell refers to him[104]—was Congressman E. G. Spaulding, a banker from Buffalo. [105]

Third, the bankers supported the legal tender legislation with unhesitating enthusiasm. The legal tender notes would, and did, allow them to replenish their legal reserves after the suspension of specie payments. The notes did serve as the foundation of a heavy extension of notes and deposits, a fact criticized by Chase and Sherman (see n. 90).

Fourth, and most important, Lincoln in his note to Congress

of January 19, 1863, criticized further issues of greenbacks, although he signed the bill authorizing an additional $100 million of them. What President Lincoln wanted was a national banking system which would enable the federal government to unify and utilize the "resources" of the banks, i.e., the fractional reserve process. Here are Lincoln's words concerning "Lincoln money":

> While giving approval [to a further issue of $100 million], however, I think it my duty to express my sincere regret that it has been found necessary to authorize so large an additional issue of United States notes, when this circulation and that of the suspended banks [meaning the suspension of specie payments] together have become already so redundant as to increase prices beyond real values, thereby augmenting the cost of living to the injury of labor, and the cost of living of the whole country.
>
> It seems very plain that continued issues of United States notes, without any check to the issues of suspended banks, and without adequate provision for the raising of money by loans, and for funding the issues so as to keep them within due limits, must soon produce disastrous consequences. And this matter appears to me so important that I feel bound to avail myself of this occasion to ask the special attention of Congress to it.[106]

He then proposed the national banking system, which was approved on February 25, 1863, one year to the day after the approval of the first Greenback Act.

It would seem safe to say, then, that Lincoln was not murdered by a paid hireling of the International Banking Conspiracy, as argued so implausibly by "Dr. R. E. Search" in *Lincoln Money Martyred* (Omni, 1935, 1965). Lincoln money was martyred, all right; it was martyred the day Abraham Lincoln signed the National Bank Act of 1863, the legislation he had been pushing for in the first place.

NOTES

[1]On the sociological distinction between power and authority, see Robert A. Nisbet, *The Social Bond* (New York: Knopf, 1970), pp. 142 ff.; Nisbet, *The Sociological Tradition* (New York: Basic Books, 1966), Ch. 4.

[2]Ethelbert Stauffer, *Christ and the Caesars* (Philadelphia: Westminster Press, 1955), p. 36.

[3]Ibid., p. 38.

[4]Ibid.

[5]Ibid., pp. 55-56.

[6]Nisbet, *Tradition and Revolt* (New York: Random House, 1968), p. 163.

[7]R. J. Rushdoony, *Politics of Guilt and Pity* (Nutley, N.J.: Craig Press, 1970); Nisbet, *The Quest for Community* (New York: Oxford University Press [1st ed., 1953] 1969).

[8]F. A. Hayek, *The Road to Serfdom* (Chicago: University of Chicago Press, 1944), Ch. 10.

[9]The portraits of Lincoln and Secretary of the Treasury Salmon P. Chase appeared on some of the U.S. Notes in 1862 and 1863 (Lincoln: $5; Chase: $1). However, when Spencer Clark, chief clerk of the National Currency Division of the Treasury, had his own portrait placed on half a million 5 cent notes ("shinplasters"), Representative Russell Thayer thought he had gone too far. He introduced the prohibiting legislation, which then passed and is still in force. On the story of the prohibition, see William P. Donlon, *United States Large Size Paper Money, 1861 to 1923* 2d ed. (Iola, Wis.: Krause, 1970), p. 17.

[10]Gary Palmer, "Still Saving Kennedy Halves?" *COINage* (September 1969): 7.

[11]Gerald T. Dunne, *Monetary Decisions of the Supreme Court* (New Brunswick, N.J.: Rutgers University Press, 1960), Preface.

[12]Jackson to Lewis (July 16, 1820); cited by Charles G. Sellers, "Banking and Politics in Jackson's Tennessee," *Mississippi Valley Historical Review* (now the *Journal of American History*), 41 (1954): 76.

[13]Jackson to Benton (n.d.); cited in ibid., p. 77. See also Jackson's State of the Union Message (December 5, 1836); reprinted in Herman E. Krooss (ed.), *Documentary History of Banking and Currency in the United States* (New York: Chelsea House and

McGraw-Hill, 1969), II, 974.

[14]Murray N. Rothbard, *The Panic of 1819* (New York: Columbia University Press, 1962), p. 188.

[15]Daniel Webster, Speech Calling for the Repeal of the Specie Circular, December 21, 1836; in *Documentary History*, II, 1027.

[16]William Gouge, *A Short History of Paper Money and Banking in the United States* (Philadelphia: T. W. Usteck, 1833), p. 171. In part reprinted in *Documentary History*, II, 904-905.

[17]Benton, cited by Hugh Rockoff, "Money, Prices, and Banks in the Jacksonian Era," in Robert W. Fogel and Stanley L. Engerman (eds.), *The Reinterpretation of American Economic History* (New York: Harper & Row, 1971), p. 448.

[18]Ibid., p. 457. The inflation came from increased specie, multiplied by fractional reserve banking. It came from abroad.

[19]Roger B. Taney [pronounced Tawney], Treasury Report on the "Removal" of Government Deposits from the Bank of the United States, December 3, 1833; in *Documentary History*, II, 966.

[20]Bray Hammond, *Sovereignty and an Empty Purse* (Princeton, N.J.: Princeton University Press, 1970), p. 19n.

[21]Taney, in *Documentary History*, II, 955.

[22]Benton (1832), in *Documentary History*, II, 811.

[23]Benton, *Thirty Years' View* (New York: Appleton, 1854), I, 201. For a similar critique of limited liability corporations, see the comments of the late nineteenth century southern Presbyterian theologian (and Stonewall Jackson's pastor) Robert L. Dabney, *Discussions: Philosophical* (Richmond, Va.: Presbyterian Committee on Publications, 1892), III, 329 ff. Cf. Rushdoony, "Limited Liability and Unlimited Money," *Politics of Guilt and Pity*, pp. 254 ff.

[24]Pure laissez-faire has never existed, but Henry Boude's comment is accurate: "Before the Civil War, government intervention in economic life was widespread but it was concentrated at the state level." Boude, "The Role of the State in American Economic Development, 1820-1890" (1959), in Thomas C. Cochran and Thomas B. Brewer (eds.), *Views of American Economic Growth: The Agricultural Era* (New York: McGraw-Hill, 1966), p. 127.

[25]Stanley Coben and Forest G. Hill have included three very telling articles illustrating this point in their book, *American Economic History: Essays in Interpretation* (Philadelphia:

Lippincott, 1966): Robert A. Lively, "The American System: A Review Article," *Business History Review* 29 (March 1955); Carter Goodrich, "American Development Policy: The Case of Internal Improvements," *Journal of Economic History* 16 (December 1956); Forest G. Hill, "Formative Relations of American Enterprise, Government and Science," *Political Science Quarterly* 75 (September 1960). Hill focuses primarily on the army corps of engineers.

[26]Hammond, *Sovereignty*, p. 17. Cf. p. 357 for a summary of Jacksonian thought.

[27]Glyndon G. Van Deusen, "Some Aspects of Whig Thought and Theory in the Jacksonian Period," *American Historical Review* 63 (January 1958); reprinted in Edward Pessen (ed.), *New Perspectives in Jacksonian Parties and Politics* (Boston: Allyn & Bacon, 1969), p. 140.

[28]Ibid., p. 154.

[29]Ibid., p. 155.

[30]Message by President Martin Van Buren on the "Economic Revulsion," of 1837, September 4, 1837; *Documentary History*, II, 1070.

[31]Sidney Fine, *Laissez Faire and the General-Welfare State* (Ann Arbor, Mich.: University of Michigan Press [1956], 1964), p. 25.

[32]Carter Goodrich, in Coben and Hill, *Essays*, p. 201.

[33]Fine, op. cit., pp. 19-20. His list of federal interventions into the economy indicates how desperate modern historians are to attribute twentieth-century concepts of government planning to pre-Civil War national political life.

[34]Reginald McGrane, "Some Aspects of American State Debts in the Forties," *American Historical Review* 38 (July 1933); in Cochran and Brewer, *Views*, pp. 165 ff.

[35]Thomas C. Cochran, "Did the Civil War Retard Industrialization?" (1961), in Cochran, *The Inner Revolution* (New York: Harper Torchbook, 1964). Cochran believes that the war did retard industrialization. His thesis has been challenged by Pershing Vartanian, "The Cochran Thesis: A Critique in Statistical Analysis," *American Historical Review* 51 (June 1964). Vartanian argues that Cochran selected misleading years to present his series, often chose the wrong products to prove his point, and overemphasized the use of statistics, especially flawed statistics from that era, in the writing of

history. He does not say that Cochran is absolutely wrong, but only that he does not prove his case. Vartanian thinks that the war merely continued the trend toward industrialization already in progress in the 1850s. A less impressive critique is Stephen Salsbury's essay, "The Effect of the Civil War on American Industrial Development," in Ralph Andreano (ed.), *The Economic Impact of the American Civil War* (Cambridge, Mass.: Schenkman, 1962), pp. 161-168.

[36]Irwin Unger, *The Greenback Era* (Princeton, N.J.: Princeton University Press, 1964), p. 13.

[37]Walter T. K. Nugent, *The Money Question During Reconstruction* (New York: Norton, 1967), p. 22.

[38]Milton Friedman and Anna J. Schwartz, *A Monetary History of the United States, 1867-1960* (published for the National Bureau of Economic Research by Princeton University Press, 1963), p. 3.

[39]*Historical Statistics of the United States, Colonial Times to 1957* (Washington, D.C.: U.S. Government Printing Office, 1960), pp. 720-721. This book was compiled by the Bureau of the Census and is widely used.

[40]Ibid., pp. 718-719.

[41]Milton Friedman, "Price, Income, and Monetary Changes in Three Wartime Periods," *American Economic Review, Papers and Proceedings* 42 (May 1952): 624 [hereafter cited as AEcR]: "Taxes as a fraction of expenditures."

[42]Cf. Eugene M. Lerner, "Money, Prices, and Wages in the Confederacy, 1861-65," *Agricultural History* 33 (July, 1959); reprinted in Andreano, *Economic Impact*. The reason for this neglect is probably the dearth of reliable statistics for the South.

[43]Wesley C. Mitchell, *A History of the Greenbacks* (Chicago: University of Chicago Press [1903], 1960), chart, p. 179.

[44]Ibid., p. 271.

[45]Donlon, *Paper Money*, p. 15. The Secret Service was established in July 1865 to combat the counterfeiters.

[46]Friedman, *Monetary History*, pp. 4, 29.

[47]Ibid., p. 86.

[48]Friedman, *AEcR*.

[49]Cf. Louis Spadaro, "Average and Aggregates in Economics," in Mary Sennholz (ed.), *On Freedom and Free Enterprise* (Princeton, N.J.: Van Nostrand, 1956), pp. 140-160.

[50]Friedman, *AEcR*, p. 624.

[51]Mitchell, *Gold, Prices & Wages Under the Greenback Standard* (New York: Kelley [1908], 1966), p. 26.

[52]Mitchell, *History*, p. 388.

[53]Emerson D. Fite, "Agricultural Development of the West During the Civil War," *Quarterly Journal of Economics* 20 (February 1906), in Andreano, *Economic Impact*, p. 56.

[54]Mitchell, *History*, p. 344.

[55]Ibid., p. 305.

[56]Ibid., chart, p. 304.

[57]Ibid., chart, p. 344.

[58]Mitchell, *Gold*, pp. 245 ff.

[59]Mitchell, *History*, p. 351.

[60]Emerson D. Fite, *Social and Industrial Conditions in the North During the Civil War* (New York: Peter Smith, 1930), p. 136.

[61]Mitchell, *Gold*, p. 41.

[62]Reuben A. Kessel and Armen A. Alchian, "Real Wages During the Civil War: Mitchell's Data Reinterpreted," *Journal of Law and Economics* 2 (October 1959), in Fogel and Engerman, *Reinterpretation*, pp. 459-467.

[63]Mitchell, *History*, p. 270.

[64]Ibid., p. 279.

[65]Ludwig von Mises, *Human Action* (New Haven: Yale University Press, 1949), Ch. 20. Cf. Murray Rothbard, *America's Great Depression* (Princeton, N.J.: D. Van Nostrand, 1963), reprinted by Nash Publishing Company, Los Angeles, 1971.

[66]The *Richmond Examiner* (June 3, 18, 1863) blamed the South's currency depreciation on speculators: Joseph Dorfman, *The Economic Mind in American Civilization* (New York: Kelley [1946], 1966), II, 985. Rev. Prof. Lyman Atwater, of the College of New Jersey (later Princeton), used the same argument in the North: ibid., p. 970. Secretary of the Treasury Chase, in his Annual Report of 1862, blamed gold speculators for driving up the price of gold, and he absolutely denied that the greenbacks were in any way at fault: *Documentary History*, II, 1346. Even Hugh McCulloch, later an outspoken foe of paper money, saw fit in his report of 1864 as Comptroller of the Currency to blame speculators for the rise in the price of gold, which in turn forced up commodity prices: ibid., II, 1421. Gold, cut loose from bank notes or government paper money,

was simply another commodity, and it had no direct impact in raising other prices.

⁶⁷Mitchell, *History*, pp. 333-334.

⁶⁸*Documentary History*, II, 1358.

⁶⁹Mitchell, *History*, pp. 334-335.

⁷⁰Hammond, *Sovereignty*, pp. 259-260.

⁷¹Simon Newcomb, *A Critical Examination of Our Financial Policy during the Southern Rebellion* (New York: Greenwood [1865], 1969), p. 114.

⁷²Cited in Hammond, *Sovereignty*, p. 204.

⁷³*Documentary History*, II, 1269.

⁷⁴Vallandigham (February 3, 1862): ibid., II, 1284.

⁷⁵Crisfield (February 5, 1862): ibid., II, 1287.

⁷⁶See my essay, "Downward Price Flexibility and Economic Growth," *The Freeman* (May 1971); reprinted in Gary North, *An Introduction to Christian Economics* (Nutley, N.J.: Craig Press, 1973), Ch. 9.

⁷⁷Newcomb, *Critical Examination*, pp. 38 ff., 42.

⁷⁸Ibid., pp. 127-128.

⁷⁹Crisfield, *Documentary History*, II, 1290.

⁸⁰Newcomb, *Critical Examination*, p. 98.

⁸¹Hammond, *Sovereignty*, pp. 259-260.

⁸²Newcomb, *Critical Examination*, p. 20.

⁸³Stephens (January 22, 1862); cited by Hammond, *Sovereignty*, p. 193.

⁸⁴Stephens (February 8, 1862): *Documentary History*, II, 1297.

⁸⁵Timothy Howe (February 12, 1862): ibid., II, 1304.

⁸⁶Ibid., II, p. 1308.

⁸⁷Newcomb, *Critical Examination*, p. 11. The South, it should be noted, did not declare its currency a legal tender: Hammond, *Sovereignty*, p. 256. However, unlike the North, the South did impose price and wage controls until shortly before the end of the war, when they were found to be too disrupting: Dorfman, *Economic Mind*, II, 987.

⁸⁸Friedman, *Monetary History*, pp. 58 ff.

⁸⁹Sherman (February 13, 1862): *Documentary History*, II, 1313.

⁹⁰Sherman (February 10, 1863): ibid., II, 1359. Cf. Chase, *Annual Report* (1862): ibid., II, 1348.

⁹¹Hammond, *Sovereignty*, p. 246.

[92]Sherman, *Documentary History*, II, 1316-1317.

[93]Ibid., II, 1317-1318.

[94]Sherman (February 10, 1863): ibid., II, 1369.

[95]Hammond, *Sovereignty*, p. 140.

[96]Newcomb, *Critical Examination*, pp. 100-101. (Cited as the introduction to this paper.)

[97]Hammond, *Sovereignty*, pp. 226-227.

[98]Ludwig von Mises, "Stones into Bread, The Keynesian Miracle," in Henry Hazlitt (ed.), *The Critics of Keynesian Economics* (Princeton, N.J.: D. Van Nostrand, 1960), pp. 305-315, makes the same point with respect to the inflationary economic proposals of Keynes.

[99]Unger, *Greenback Era*, Ch. 6.

[100]Cf. my essay, "Gertrude Coogan and the Myth of Social Credit," in North, *Introduction to Christian Economics*, Ch. 11.

[101]Hammond, *Sovereignty*, p. 24.

[102]Annual Treasury Report (1861): *Documentary History*, II, 1343; Mitchell, *History*, pp. 62, 68 ff.

[103]Annual Treasury Report (1862): ibid., II, 1350.

[104]Mitchell, *History*, index, p. 575; cf. p. 70.

[105]On Spaulding's occupation as a banker, see Dorfman, *Economic Mind*, II, 972-973.

[106]*Congressional Globe*, 37th Congress, 3d Session, pp. 392-393.

8

Hard Money and Society in the Bible

ROUSAS JOHN RUSHDOONY

President, Chalcedon, Canoga Park, California

For all too many academicians of our time, the ultimate in scholarly pornography is to think in Christian theistic or biblical terms. The militantly humanistic scholarship of our time has a tabu on such an approach and is informed by a religious humanism. However, since our civilization is a product of twenty centuries of biblical faith and law, it is important for us, in analyzing our monetary crisis, to understand the biblical framework of our heritage.

Biblical law speaks of money, not in terms of coinage, but as *weight*. Leviticus 19: 35-37 declares:

> Ye shall do no unrighteousness in judgment, in mete-yard, in weight, or in measure.

Just balances, just weights, a just ephah, and a just hin,
shall ye have: I am the LORD your God, which brought
you out of the land of Egypt.

Therefore shall ye observe all my statutes, and all my
judgments, and do them: I am the LORD.

The significance of the term *weights* has been lost on us in
recent years because of our custom of regarding money
primarily as a paper currency, and secondarily as coinage. Not
only was coinage a late development of the monetary scene,
and paper currency a modern development, but, long after the
appearance of gold and silver coins, monetary exchange was
governed by weights of gold and silver. Bush, in commenting
on Leviticus 19: 35-37, wrote:

Ye shall do no unrighteousness in judgment. The word
"judgment" in this connexion is very plausibly referred by
the Hebrew writers to all the particulars that follow. On
this construction it is held, that Moses uses the word here
in order to intimate of what solemn moment he would
have the law considered, which relates to true measures
and weights. The man that falsified either was to be
regarded as a *corrupter of judgment*, an emphatic
designation, equivalent to vile, wicked, abominable in a
very high degree———. In mete-yard. Heb. *bammiddah;* a
measure of *length* or *surface*, such as the yard, cubit, foot,
span, &c.———*In weight.* Heb. *bamishkol;* such as the
talent, shekel, & c.—*In measure.* Heb. *bammesurah;* by
which is denoted measures of capacity, such as the homer,
ephah, seah, hin, &c. In all these articles, as well as in the
balances or scales, weight-stones, &c., mentioned in the
next verse, they were to observe the most honest
exactness, and never allow themselves to practise any
species of fraud in their dealings and commerce, because
they might not think it of easy detection.[1]

That *weights* meant money was once well known. Thus, *Fairbairn's Bible Encyclopedia* (1866) discusses the shekel under the classification of *weights*. The Bible speaks of money as a *weight*. For example, we are told that "David gave to Ornan for the place six hundred shekels of gold by weight" (I Chronicles 21: 25); in other words, the payment was made in terms of a specified weight of gold. In Isaiah 33: 18, Lowth translates, "Where is he now, the accountant? where the weigher of tribute?" The Berkeley Version reads, "Where is the weigher?" The reference is to the payment of tribute by weight, apparently by Hezekiah to Sennacherib. From the days of Abraham to at least the time of Hezekiah, money meant gold and silver, ready cut and weighed.

While we have no direct evidence of the weight of the Hebrew shekel as cited in the law of Moses, we do have enough data from later sources, Josephus in particular, to construct a table of weights. Kennedy gave us a table of the weights[2] from the conquest of Canaan to the extinction of the Jewish nation, the weight being listed to the nearest large fraction:

	Gold Standard	
	Heavy	*Light*
Shekel	$252\frac{2}{3}$ grs. troy	$126\frac{1}{3}$ grs.
Mina 50 shekels	12,630 grs. troy	6,315 grs.
Talent 3000 shekels	758,000 grs. troy	379,000 grs.
	Silver Standard	
Shekel	$224\frac{1}{2}$ grs. troy	$112\frac{1}{4}$ grs.
Mina 50 shekels	11,225 grs. troy	5,660 grs.
Talent 3000 shekels	673,500 grs. troy	336,750 grs.

The ordinary or heavy gold shekel, weighing 252 2/3 grains troy, was thus a little more in weight than two modern British sovereigns, the weight of the sovereign being 123.274 grains troy.

Early coinage, while still called by various names, such as drachma or trahm, was still governed by weight. As a matter of fact, the Puritan and bibilically oriented nature of early America led to a return to weight. Not all colonial coinage carried a denomination; although called shillings, groats, and pence, these terms did not usually appear on the coins. The first gold coin actually struck for the United States was the half eagle or $5 gold piece, which, from 1795 to 1806, did not bear any mark of value. The Coinage Act of April 2, 1792, required simply that the coin weigh 135 grains, 916 2/3 fine. The weight was changed by the Act of June 28, 1834, to 129 grains, 899.225 fine, and, finally, fineness became, by the Act of January 18, 1837, .900. The early eagles ($10 gold) also carried no denomination until 1838. The silver trade dollar, issued for circulation in the Orient (1873-1885), carried the denomination "Trade Dollar" and also the weight, "420 grains 900 Fine."[3] The most popular of all coins, the famous Austrian Maria Theresa thaler, never carried a denomination but was used in almost every continent as a weight of silver. In the United States, some of the private "coinage" was merely a weight of gold. Thus, Moffat & Company of San Francisco was the most important of the California private coiners. From 1849 to 1853, Moffat issued small rectangular pieces of gold in values from $9.43 to $264. The known surviving types are the $9.43, $14.25, and $16 ingots. The face of the $14.25 ingot read, "Moffat & Co., 21 3/4 carat, $14.25," and the other side listed the weight and grains.

In terms of biblical law, honest money is honest weight, in gold or silver. James Moffat, in his translation of the Bible, rendered Leviticus 19: 35, "You must never act dishonestly, in court or in commerce, as you use measures of length, weight, or capacity."[4] Biblical law, in its case law specifics, forbids fractional reserve.[5] It also regards all departures from money as weight as fraud and counterfeiting, and as part of a broader pattern of apostasy and moral collapse. This appears plainly, for example, in Isaiah's citation of God's bill of indictment against Judah and Jerusalem, whereby judgment will overwhelm them. According to Isaiah 1: 21-24,

21. How is the faithful city become an harlot! it was full of judgment; righteousness lodged in it; but now murderers.

22. Thy silver is become dross, thy wine mixed with water:

23. Thy princes are rebellious, and companions of thieves: every one loveth gifts (bribes), and followeth after rewards: they judge not the fatherless, neither doth the cause of the widow come unto them.

24. Therefore saith the Lord, the LORD of hosts, the mighty ONE of Israel, Ah, I will ease me of mine adversaries, and avenge me of mine enemies.

The picture is one of a decadent and inflationary society, one in which money had become dross or refuse, the impurity in melted metal rather than the silver itself. The image of wine mixed with water not only describes adulteration but the essence of inflation. In Ezekiel 45: 9-12, God indicts false weights and calls for the removal of "violence and spoil" and the administration of civil justice, and He establishes the exact ratio of the shekel to its lesser and greater weights, as well as dealing with balances and measures of capacity. As a result, Crawford Toy, writing in "Proverbs" (p. 324) from a liberal viewpoint, states frankly, that, in the text of Scripture, "God is the ordainer of the machinery of commercial transactions."[6] This is not a condition which sets well with modern man. But let us examine its implications and context.

First, as we have seen, God's requirement, according to the Bible, is that money must be in terms of a weight of gold or silver. This is required because justice calls for full value at all times. To short-weight a man either in selling him grain or money is theft, and the law declares plainly, "Thou shalt not steal" (Exodus 20: 15). A false weight or shekel of gold or silver is "spoil" or "despoiling the people" and is contrary to "law and justice" (Moffat's rendering, Ezekiel 45: 9).

Second, a very limited state is allowed by biblical law, and its taxing power is limited to a head tax, or poll tax, on all males over twenty years of age, and the same for all (Exodus 30: 11-16). The basic social financing is not by the state, but by means of the tithe, which finances religion, education, health, welfare, etc.[7]

Third, biblical law has no prison system but rather requires restitution. A thief restores the thing stolen, plus a penalty, from double the value of the article to four- or five-fold, depending on the nature of the item. Thus, "If a man shall steal an ox, or a sheep, and kill it, or sell it; he shall restore five oxen for an ox, and four sheep for a sheep" (Exodus 22: 1). Sheep have an income potential as a source of wool, as meat, and for breeding, so that more than double restitution is required. Oxen were valuable for their meat and hide, and very important as well-trained beasts of burden, capable of hauling greater weight than horses; hence, their value was greater. Crime thus did not pay: full value had to be restored; the habitual criminal had to be executed.

The goal of the law was thus *restitution*, where offenses occurred (full value retained for property), and *full value* in all monetary transactions by requiring a standard and unchanging weight of gold and silver as the medium of exchange. Not only is hard money the standard of Scripture, but it is plainly declared to be the law of God. This is a very serious consideration. It accounts for the persistence, in times of a biblically governed faith, of a demand for hard money. Insufficient attention has been paid to the critique of debased coinage by the early Church Fathers. The reformers were also aware of the problem. Thus, Luther, in commenting on God's judgment on all sinners in his key work, the *Commentary on the Epistle to the Romans*, declared, with respect to Romans 2: 2, 3, that

> Today we may apply the Apostle's words first to those (*rulers*) who without cogent cause inflict exorbitant taxes upon the people, or by changing and devaluating the currency, rob them, while at the same time they accuse their subjects of being greedy and avaricious. Even worse are the blinded ecclesiastical rulers who commit similar, if not greater wrongs as everybody knows.[8]

Rulers have not changed much since Luther's day. They still debase the currency and blame the people for the resulting inflation.

Matthew Henry (1662-1714) said of Leviticus 19: 35-37, "He that sells, is bound to give the full of the commodity, and he that buys, the full of the price agreed upon, which cannot be done without just balances, weights, and measures."[9]

It is clear, from the foregoing, that the kind of society that biblical law calls for has a certain rigidity of framework with respect to values. God's unchanging law governs all things, and God requires that all weights and measures represent His requirement, that they be full value. The matter can be expressed thus: a modern definition of money has it that money is a representation of wealth or property. This is a fair definition of a paper currency: it is a representation of wealth, not the real thing, and its value is fluid and changeable. In terms of the biblical requirement, money cannot be a representation of wealth: it must be wealth, so that all transactions should be exchanges of wealth, not of real wealth for a symbol or representation of wealth.

Biblical law thus has a rigid framework in order that men may have freedom within that framework, and so that productivity can flourish without penalty as a result of that framework.

Something of the significance of this fact appears in a statement by John Sherman, a prominent American statesman of the last half of the nineteenth century, who, unfortunately, is best remembered for the Sherman Anti-Trust Act. In a Senate speech on February 27, 1865, Sherman said in part:

> We cannot fix the price or value of any commodity, whether Gold, Silver, or Food. The attempt has been made by many Governments in different ages, and has uniformly failed. The standard of value may be fixed by the Government, but a higher Law (Economic Law) fixes the relative value of all commodities as measured by this standard. We may as well recognize as an axiom of political economy, proven by the experience of Nations, by every form of Government—Despotic, Monarchic, or Republican—that the fixing of the values of commodities is beyond the power of legislation. We may fix the Standard of Value, we may fix the Tax upon the commodity, and there our power ends. And especially is this so of Gold, which has value in all civilized nations of the world; and, except with Nations for a time involved in War, is everywhere the Standard of Value. It is therefore manifest that the first duty of Congress is to keep our lawful money, as a Standard of Value, as near as possible to the Standard of Gold.[10]

The biblical premise is that the law framework is constant, and that men are not. Men change, and productivity changes, but not the basic rules of God concerning man, money, commerce, and life in general. The framework is rigid and constant in order to provide man freedom within that framework.

How strongly this standard persisted is apparent in the Talmud. Coming many centuries later than the law, and with the use of debased coinage commonplace by that time in one nation after another, the Talmud is still plainly dedicated to a hard money standard. The rabbinic lawyers whose commentaries make up the Talmud were sometimes firmly faithful to the word of the law, and, at other times, like the U.S. Supreme Court today, very much given to exploiting the wording of the law to push it to very alien conclusions from its original meaning. With respect to money, however, the Talmud raises essentially one question: a gold standard, or a silver standard? Shall gold be established as the standard, and silver regarded as a product, or vice versa? The debate was waged by the rabbis over this issue. For example, we read the following, with respect to the opinion of one leading authority, R. Judah the Prince:

> Rabbi taught his son R. Simeon: Gold acquires silver. Said he to him: Master, in your youth you did teach us, Silver acquires gold; now, advanced in age, you reverse it and teach, Gold acquires silver. Now, how did he reason in his youth, and how did he reason in his old age?—In his youth he reasoned: Since gold is more valuable, it ranks as money; whilst silver, which is of lesser value, is regarded as produce: hence (the delivery of) produce effects a title to the money. But at a later age he reasoned: Since silver (coin) is current, it ranks as money; whilst gold, which is not current, is accounted as produce, and so the produce effects a title to the money.[11]

This is a revealing fact. The strait-jacket of the law was seen as so binding money to gold and silver that the only possible open question for the Talmudic lawyers was their relationship: which one set the standard? However, by requiring a strait-jacket concept of money, the law thereby provided freedom for man.

In modern society, man has declared his independence from God and from the law of God. The religious humanism which undergirds and informs life and scholarship requires that man be free from any transcendental norms, laws, principles, and restraints. The idea that laws handed down by God to Moses centuries ago should control property ("Thou shalt not steal") and fix money to the weight of a precious metal is unthinkable. Man cannot be bound to any plan of God's making.

Increasingly, the hostility is also directed against any preestablished plan, by God or man. As against the earlier socialist idea of a *planned* society, the American pragmatists advanced the idea of "a *planning* economy" rather than "a planned economy." Because a planned economy still involved some kind of fixity of economic law or theory, the pragmatists rebelled against it in favor of an experimental approach. A planned economy was seen as law-bound and past-bound, whereas a planning economy was held to be creative and makes its own conditions and laws.[12]

The revolt, thus, in the name of the freedom of man has been against the constraint of any law of God certainly, and also the laws of men. The disturbances of the second half of the twentieth century should therefore be no surprise to us. When the philosophers and educators of our era have required so radical a break with established law the consequences are sure to be drastic and/or revolutionary. That men's ideas of money should be affected is a natural consequence. It was very common during the 1930s in the United States to hear progressive educators ridicule the idea of a gold standard. Anything could be money, it was said: hay, wheat, land, or goods could provide a backing for a currency, but what better backing could a paper currency have, *if* one were needed, then the credit, productivity, and taxing power of the United States?

Endless variations of this theme can be cited. Basic to all these "funny money" concepts were two essentially religious premises. *First*, man was seen as a creator, replacing God. Man's declaration of independence from God means the supplanting of God by man. This is how the Bible presents original sin, the desire of every man to be his own god, "Knowing" or

determining good and evil in terms of himself (Genesis 3: 5).
Just as God created heaven and earth out of nothing, so man
creates values out of nothing. In Christian theology, values are
what God declares them to be. In humanism, values are what
man declares them to be. If man or the state declares that fiat
money has value, it therefore has value. The application of the
word *fiat* to money is theologically significant. It is Latin for
"Let it be done." The concept echoes Genesis 1: 3, etc., "And
God said, Let there be light: and there was light." The *fiat*
power of God has been transferred to man and applied to
money. Man is now the creative force in the world, and it is
man's word and will that governs reality, in fact *makes* reality,
and establishes values. The position of Hegel, "The rational is
the real," means that what man's autonomous reason
establishes is thus the new reality, or the reality in process of
becoming. For Marx, this meant that man now recreates the
world in terms of his rationality, because no other reality has
any meaning. In his *Theses on Feuerbach*, Marx declared,
"The philosophers have only *interpreted* the world, in various
ways; the point, however, is to *change* it." Jerry Rubin applied
the idea to the student revolutionary scene of the 1960s, declaring, "We create reality wherever we go by living our
fantasies."[13] If the rational is the real, then the intellectual elite
of statism can create fiat money in the assurance that their
ideas must work if implemented with the full force of rational
planning. It is thus a natural consequence of modern religious
humanism that man should, as his own ultimate and god, issue
fiat money, values, and laws. The logic of humanism requires
it.

Second, the logical corollary of this is that man, as his own
lawmaker now, is freed from past laws. As the new god of
being, modern statist man is no longer bound by the word of
the old God of Scripture. Perhaps it is unfair or unkind to
remind anyone that, a decade ago, when the hoarding of silver
coins began, there were those who insisted that Gresham's law
was no longer operative. That it did operate, some hold, was

because too many men were still governed by reactionary concepts. Given sufficient re-education away from the ostensible myths of hard money, man, it is held, will no longer operate as though classical economics were true, or as though God ordained hard money in His law. Re-educated man, it is maintained, will be free from past laws and will be able to prosper under fiat money. The presupposition of this position is that there is no reality beyond the mind of man. It presupposes an economic Christian Science: the only reality is Mind, and what the elite planning Mind decrees is ipso facto reality. However, no more than a universal belief in Christian Science would eliminate toothaches and broken bones will a belief in a Christian Science Economics eliminate the consequences of fiat money.

As against the rigid framework of biblical law (money as weight, a hard money policy), the modern socialistic view of money is notable for its freedom from any standard, its lack of association with weight and with an established value. This does not mean that rigidity or fixity is absent from the new economics. It has simply been transferred from money to man. Biblical law, by controlling the definition of money and limiting it to weights of gold and silver, thereby freed man for the free exercise of productivity and change. Modern economics, by "freeing" money from an objective norm and weight, has transferred rigidity and controls to man. The closer we get to purely fiat money, the more rigid and pervasive the controls.

Moreover, fiat money is simply *political* money. It is a creature of the state and a captive of the state. Since the life-blood of economics is money, to make money political is to surrender economics and man's wealth and properties into the hands of the state. The freedom of the new economics becomes slavery. Very simply, managed money means managed men. As Rist observed, "We shall have sound money, or we shall cease to be free."[14] The alternative then is hard money or a hard dictatorship.[15]

The history of the American colonies is very instructive as to the goals of paper money. Central to its purpose was economic warfare. The mercantilist economics of England placed the colonies in a very difficult position. Their role was to provide both raw materials for England and a market for English goods. There was legislation against the development of manufacturing in the colonies, as well as restrictions on trade with other countries. Thus, the Yankee ships in trading with countries who could sell more cheaply to them were usually guilty of smuggling. The earliest issue, in Massachusetts Bay Colony in 1690, was to pay for military expenditures in King William's War (1690-1697), and a 5 percent premium was granted to those who might use them for tax payments as an incentive to acceptance. This and other early emissions were called "bills of credit" rather than money. However, these emissions were soon put to a very aggressive use.

The necessity of trading with the mother country penalized the colonies. The colonies, however loyal to the mother country, resented the economic penalties. English governors of American colonies were instructed to deny approval to any American law passed without a governor's consent, and to all legislation involving paper money except in a military emergency. The crown also retained the right of veto over all measures passed with a governor's consent. This veto, however, only became effective when the measure in question was reported to London and the veto relayed to the colony. Obviously, this meant the passage of more than a little time in those days. The colonies, New England in particular, took advantage of this fact. By passing paper emissions, they were able to use them until such time as the royal veto returned from London. Until then, all English merchants, with their resented privileges, could be paid off, despite their protests, with paper money. "English merchants constantly pressured the Crown to stiffen control of paper money, and the colonists constantly urged that they should be permitted to handle their own monetary affairs."[16]

It is beyond our purpose here to trace the subsequent

history of paper issues. Between 1740 and 1750, in New England the issues went out of control, and Parliament passed an act, effective September 29, 1751, providing strict control over all future issues. What is relevant to our purpose is the fact that, *first*, the paper emission, after its early emergency military use, became an instrument of economic reprisals and warfare against a mercantilist economy and the restrictions it imposed on the colonies. This was particularly true of New England. Because they had been penalized by mercantilism, they were determined to penalize the English merchants in return. Paper emissions were an ideal instrument for economic warfare. *Second*, the utility of such paper money caught on in other areas. Debtors at once realized that they could pay off their own debts with this cheap money, and they quickly took advantage of the fact. Paper emissions gained a rapid popularity among the debtor classes of the colonies. With them also it was a form of economic warfare. Thus, what began as an action against English merchants became a popular action against American merchants and creditors. It was this background, together with the desire to cleanse the country of the economic warfare created by paper money, that led to the hard money requirement of the U.S. Constitution.

The same considerations are still pertinent today. Paper money does provide an ideal instrument for economic warfare and a means of furthering a conflict of interests. The debtor classes today include most of all the major corporations, as well as all peoples of all classes who are consumption-oriented and in debt. Most of all, however, the state is able to wage economic warfare against all classes, against capital and labor, because it is the creator of fiat money and always controls the freshest and cheapest supply of money. It thereby has an instrument of confiscation of capital and values and is the strongest contender in the economic war. The term *warfare state*, coined a few years ago and applied to the so-called military-industrial complex, applies better to the paper money state. By its emissions of paper money, or fractional reserve currencies, a state declares war on its people and promotes economic warfare between debtors and creditors. Economic progress is hindered by paper money and is progressively crippled.

On the other hand, few appreciate sufficiently the rule of gold and silver in the extension of trade and commerce throughout Europe after the fall of Rome, and in the development of cities. The studies of Agus have shown the key role of Jewish merchants in the development of urban civilization in pre-Crusade Europe, especially during the tenth and eleventh centuries. These men were "very conservative and punctilious in their religious observances." As the merchants of Europe, they gained privileges because their role was so important to society.

These few Jews forced the prelates of the Church to become their protectors, and the rulers and nobles to become their benefactors. In the midst of almost universal personal subjugation, the Jews alone were politically free; in the midst of turbulence and war, they alone could travel in comparative safety and could carry valuable merchandise over long distances. When practically every man owed to his superior services and dues that constituted a sacrifice of from fifteen to fifty per cent of his income-producing time, the Jews paid as taxes but a tiny fraction of their income. They organized self-governing communities, developed supra communal institutions, enacted ordinances on a national scale, and employed a most efficient and most remarkable form of group organization and group government, one that afforded every individual effective help and protection even when he was hundreds of miles away from home. They instituted practices and procedures that gave them great power and resilience, enabled them to deal with the princes of Church and state from a position of strength, and created for them opportunities for powerful economic growth and great physical expansion.[17]

These Jewish merchants were the bourgeoisie of Europe and constituted a privileged class precisely because of the service they rendered. Modern nationalism has obscured the primitivism of the European peoples after the fall of Rome, and especially such facts as human sacrifice. Charlemagne found it necessary to resort to strong measures to stamp it out in one area of his realm. The readiness of these peoples, in this earlier era, to recognize the value of merchants was important to their growth and development. According to Agus, "The taxes the Jews of the period paid to their overlords, usually amounted to about two or three percent of their active capital."[18] The Jewish merchants governed their affairs by reference to the Torah and followed the biblical requirement of hard money. The European coinage of the period was of silver. However, Moslem gold coins and Byzantine gold coins circulated to a degree in Europe.[19] The various coins were differently valued, and thus required exchange standards in terms of their actual weight of gold and silver. Not infrequently, coins were reduced to weight and used as weights of gold and silver, both for trade and for storage. Wills paid to heirs sums of these pounds of hard money, and we find from them that "A pound of gold consisted of twelve pounds of silver."[20]

At a later date, the Code of Maimonodes reveals the careful attention given to hard money, and the existence of a silver standard because of the comparative scarcity of silver. Thus, we are told that "gold denars have the status of a commodity vis-a-vis silver coins, and likewise, copper ma'ah have the status of a commodity vis-a-vis silver coins."[21]

Byzantium, however, was the central area of wealth and commerce for centuries, and it was essentially a commercial civilization whose traders reached the far outposts of the known world. The money of Byzantium was exclusively gold and copper. Byzantium had a doubly important heritage: the biblical emphasis on money as weight and the Greek demand for hard money during most of ancient Hellenic history. As Groseclose observed, of Byzantium and its monetary standard:

> During the long period of Byzantine history, foreign trade was an important source of social income . . . Though Byzantine gold moved out to the most distant corners of the earth and served as the measure of value to feudatories in England and to Persian merchants in India, there was no apparent diminution of supplies at Constantinople, no scarcity of metal that would provoke an alteration of the standard.
> The fact is that Byzantium did not concern itself with "mercantilism." In both the early and later Greek civilization an economic structure was built upon money, but money was kept as a means rather than as an object of commercial activity. Property arose from the growth of natural rather than monetary wealth, and financial activity was concerned with the acquisition and movement of physical rather than monetary values.[22]

Byzantium regarded two things as essential to its existence: orthodoxy, or sound Christianity, and gold coinage, or sound money. In fact, Cosmas, the Sailor of the Indies, held that these two elements accounted for the prosperity of Byzantine commerce. Modern scholars are apt to smile at this association, but there was a biblical premise for sound coinage which governed Byzantine thinking. For over six centuries, from Constantine I (d. 337 A.D.) to Nicephorus III, Botaniates (1076-1081), who reduced the amount of gold in the coin, the Byzantine coinage retained its value unimpaired. Defeat at the hands of the Turks at the Battle of Manzikert in 1071, was the excuse for tampering with the coinage. The world lost its "one reliable medium of exchange. Constantinople was no longer the financial centre of the world."[23] The steady collapse thereafter of the Byzantine coinage brought international financial chaos. As Runciman observed,

> Indeed, the days of the Palaeologi are a sad last chapter to the Empire. The coinage that the King of Ceylon liked above all others was now dishonoured even in Pera. The merchandise that paid rich tolls at the wharves of Constantinople was carried past her walls now by the Genoese without calling or travelled by a far-away route by Syria and ships of Venice. Her situation was valueless now, and her monetary pride humbled and discarded. The tragedy of the long death of Byzantium is above all a financial tragedy.[24]

The sad fact is that the same tragedy is being reenacted today. The issues are essentially the same, and the same is true of the principles at stake.

NOTES

[1]George Bush, *Notes, Critical and Practical, on the Book of Leviticus* (New York: Ivison & Phinney, 1857), p. 214.

[2]A.R.S. Kennedy, "Money," in James Hastings, ed., *A Dictionary of the Bible* (New York: Charles Scribner's Sons, 1919), III, 419.

[3]For much valuable data on U.S. coinage, see R. S. Yeoman, *A Guide Book of United States Coins*, published annually by Western Publishing Company. The 1971 edition (p. 3), in citing the rise of the price of coins (as well as their decline at times, and the reasons why), listed first the fact that "The trend of our economy is inflationary."

[4]For more on biblical law, see R. J. Rushdoony, *Institutes of Biblical Law* (Nutley, N.J.: The Presbyterian & Reformed Publishing Company, 1972).

[5]See Gary K. North, *Introduction to Christian Economics* (Nutley, N.J.: Craig Press, 1973).

[6]Cited in Charles T. Fritsch, "Proverbs," in *The Interpreter's Bible* (New York: Abingdon Press, 1955), IV, 874.

[7]See R. J. Rushdoony, *Institutes of Biblical Law.*

[8]Martin Luther, *Commentary on the Epistle to the Romans* (Grand Rapids, Mich.: Zondervan, 1954), Mueller translation, p. 37.

[9]Matthew Henry, *A Commentary on the Holy Bible* (New York: Funk & Wagnalls, n.d.), I, 306.

[10]Cited by Franklyn Hobbes, *Gold, the Real Ruler of the World* (Chicago: The Business Foundation Publishers, 1943), p. 177 f.

[11]Baba Mezi'a, Ch. IV, in *The Babylonian Talmud*, Seder Nezikin (London: The Soncino Press, 1935), I, 263.

[12]See Harold Ordway Rugg, *The Great Technology, Social Chaos and the Public Mind* (New York: John Day, 1933), especially Ch. IX.

[13]Jerry Rubin, *Do It!* (New York: Simon and Schuster, 1970), p. 143.

[14]Charles Rist, *The Triumph of Gold*, Philip Cortney, translator (New York: Philosophical Library, 1961), p. 2.

[15]See R. J. Rushdoony, *Politics of Guilt and Pity* (Nutley, N.J.: Craig Press, 1970), p. 209.

[16]Eric P. Newman, *The Early Paper Money of America* (Racine, Wis.: Whitman Publishing Company, 1967), p. 11.

[17]Irving A. Agus, *Urban-Civilization in Pre-Crusade Europe* (New York: Yeshiva University Press, 1968), I, 16 f.

[18]Ibid., I, 17.

[19]Ibid., I, 96, 146, 264, 278.

[20]Ibid., II, 719 f.

[21]Isaac Kelin, translator, *The Code of Maimonodes, Book Twelve, The Book of Acquisitions* (New Haven: Yale University Press [1951], 1955), p. 24.

[22]Elgin Groseclose, *Money: The Human Conflict* (Norman, Okla.: University of Oklahoma Press, 1934), p. 151.

[23]Steven Runciman, *Byzantine Civilisation* (London: Edward Arnold [1933], 1936), p. 53.

[24]Ibid., p. 178.

9

Is the Gold Standard Gone Forever?

ARTHUR KEMP

Professor of Economics, Claremont Men's College

To attempt an answer to such a question, involving as it must both prescription and prediction, requires some understanding of what the term *gold standard* really means. The same label has been applied to very different kinds of arrangements, some of which could be established or reestablished rather easily while others would be most difficult, if not impossible. Some advocates of what is called a gold standard, for example, consider a 100 percent private gold money as the only true gold standard; others are willing to settle for the use of gold in its international functions alone; still others insist on applying the term only to a system permitting and fostering redemption in terms of gold bullion or gold coin both domestically and internationally. Whichever type of gold standard one chooses, an understanding requires a close study of the essential circumstances which led to gold becoming *the* most important monetary metal in the history of the world.

It should be emphasized at the beginning that gold has had widespread usage both in its artistic and monetary functions since very ancient times. Whether or not we can pinpoint the beginning, it seems clear that it has been in widespread use since at least 5000-3000 B.C., and very possibly even before that. Early civilizations, widely separated from each other both in space and in time, admired gold and used it not only in the arts but also as a measure of wealth and as a medium of exchange. I shall not argue purely from the historical evidence. That gold has played a very important role in the past is not sufficient justification for its continued use in the present. But, even if one accepts the argument (which I do not) that the monetary use of gold is the result of nothing more than superstition, ignorance, myth, and illusion, the historical significance of gold in monetary affairs cannot be disregarded. Myths have played some very important parts in the development of human affairs.

The history of the evolutionary development of gold as a monetary metal suggests that it originated in voluntary acts of individuals pursuing their private, mercantile ends. They discovered that measuring by gold weight facilitated commercial exchanges, preserved purchasing power over time, and aided in the formation of capital. Moreover, it seems clear that such usage preceded the device of coinage and was developed independently of governmental authority. In short, gold standards were not invented, but discovered. No other metal, commodity, system, or mechanism up to the present time has had the widespread acceptance as has gold, nor has any other device survived for so long the attempts to ridicule it, to confiscate it, to outlaw it. "As good as gold!" "The Golden Rule!" "Speech is silver; silence is gold!" Every modern language is filled with such picturesque phrases, most of them complimentary.

True, rulers, emperors, governments did not take long to recognize the advantages and disadvantages of gold to their own objectives and ambitions. The discovery of coining had political and religious overtones as well as very practical economic applications. To have a well-turned likeness of the ruler on coins, or the appropriate symbols sacred to the gods, must have had considerable public relations effects. It also served as a sort of certification of weight and fineness and as such has continued to the present day. With the development of more complex and sophisticated legal systems, such legal certification became the specification of the basic legal means for settling disputes involving debt, damages in the case of contracts impossible to fulfill, actions involving trespass, libel, slander, and so on. This improved the ability of government to serve as arbiter of private disputes.

Probably very early in the development, governments refused to be content with a purely secondary, passive role in monetary affairs. Perhaps it would have been better had government been denied any role whatever in monetary affairs. But the question seems to me academic at best. Virtually every country in the world, whether democratic or autocratic, assigns to government a high degree of responsibility for providing a monetary framework—and some of the decisions of the highest courts have asserted that it is an inherent and inseparable part of sovereignty. Whether one agrees or not, it is clear that governments have demonstrated again and again a remarkable ability to utilize the monetary system for the purpose of increasing their control over the real resources of the citizenry. The number and variety of socially desirable projects that governments can devise seem infinite. All require financing; lack of money is always and everywhere a hindrance. Put more properly, to carry out the projects requires government to obtain control of the necessary real resources, and one method for doing so has been control of monetary sources. Whether by the rather primitive device of debasing the coinage through clipping, sweating, or recalling and reminting, or by issuing unsecured paper money, or by the more sophisticated modern techniques of deficit financing through the central bank, the result has been to provide governments with that control. Not by coincidence, the only period of movement in the direction of some degree of decentralization of control over the monetary mechanisms took place during the liberal movement toward limited government during the eighteenth and nineteenth centuries. The only device to stem the movement toward centralization was the gold standard, and from the point of view of our century even this appears to have been temporary.

The preeminence of gold as a monetary metal was reached in the nineteenth century. Silver, prior to that time, might be considered to have been a serious rival but, for reasons that need not be discussed here, dating perhaps from the Gold Standard Act of 1816 by England, gold ascended to undisputed first place, although the champions of silver continued to drag their heels throughout the century. The gold standards, as adopted by various countries, had two aspects, one domestic, the other international. The international aspect derived from the domestic. There were also some widely different legal, institutional, and economic arrangements. But in the generic sense, these gold standards were based upon a similar legal status: (1) the monetary unit of each gold standard country was defined in terms of that unit's weight and fineness (a coinage definition); and (2) there was designated an agency, not necessarily governmental, which was instructed to buy and sell gold for money, and money for gold. Using the United States as an example, from 1834 on the pure gold content of the dollar was 23.22 grains, resulting in a mint price (480/23.22) of $20.67 an ounce.[1]

All the major moneys of the world today are, or were at one time, defined in terms of metallic weight, and the vast majority were in terms of gold and presupposed coining gold. Domestically, a gold coin standard provides for redemption of standard monetary units in gold, with the minimum amount equal to the minimum authorized coin. The device of a so-called gold bullion standard increases the size of the minimal transaction by defining the weight of a gold bar; this practice, it appears, was adopted in the hope of confining most uses of gold to the settlement of international balances. I regard the gold coin standard as the only true gold standard—*the* gold standard, so to speak—and all other variations, restrictions, modifications, and alterations as departures, both in theory and practice, from a true gold standard. All the variations, such as the gold bullion standard and the gold exchange standard, have untoward side effects restricting the functioning of the gold coin standard as it evolved historically.

The important function of gold internationally evolved from the various domestic gold coin standards in an unconscious, spontaneous, and gradual manner. It was not the result of governmental appointees meeting together in order to establish an international gold standard by political agreement. It also seems likely that the domestic success of the gold standard in providing a relatively high degree of stability of the general price level in various countries contributed to its international function as well.

It should be emphasized that, although the evidence, logic, and measurable experience indicate that the gold coin standards of the two centuries prior to 1914 were accompanied by a much greater price stability than has occurred since that time, this does not mean that no inflationary periods were present. Relatively stable price levels do not mean absolutely unchanging general price levels. But in those two centuries, the periods of extensive inflation were mainly associated with wars. In many countries, as measured by wholesale prices, the average annual variation in prices was close to 5 percent and the maximum variation was rarely above 20 percent. Moreover, in countries whose devotion to a gold coin standard was reasonably steady over the period, the price levels at the end of the period were not far different than at the beginning. To say that this is in contrast to experience since 1914, or even in the last three decades, is gross understatement.

There seems to be little dispute about the facts. In a speech delivered at Toronto, Canada, in December 1972, Arthur Burns, the chairman of the Board of Governors of the Federal Reserve System, recognized it as follows:

> The current inflationary problem has no close parallel in economic history. In the past, inflation in the United States was associated with military outlays during wars or with investment booms in peacetime. Once these episodes passed, the price level typically declined, and many years often elapsed before prices returned to their previous peak. . . .
>
> Over the past quarter century, a rather different pattern of wage and price behavior has emerged. . . . The average level of prices, however, hardly ever declines. . . .
>
> Almost the entire world is at present suffering from inflation, and in many countries—for example Canada, France, the United Kingdom, West Germany, and the Netherlands—the pace of inflation is more serious than in the United States.[2]

In these comments there is not one word of recognition that there is a tendency under a gold standard to check and reverse strong price movements in either direction. Nor is there even a recognition that this tendency operates through the restraints imposed on the total money stock. A gold coin standard, it seems, imposes too great a restriction on the discretionary powers of central bankers. Price-level stability, it is argued over and over again, is only one of several goals of monetary policy—an argument few would deny. But then it is argued that discretion and flexibility in these powers are essential to wise choices made by wise men, accompanied by direct price and wage controls. The evidence supporting the second assertion is nonexistent.

Under gold coin standards, gold functioned as a reserve against paper promises to pay, both domestically and internationally, in clearing arrangements both domestic and international, and in storing value over time. Gold resists restraints placed upon it; it is hoarded; it escapes to places government officials cannot reach; it resists manipulation by governments or central banks, even when the penalties for its possession and use are about as severe as man's ingenuity can devise.

During much of the nineteenth century, as more and more nations adopted gold standards domestically, gold performed a very significant role in relating currencies, prices, and interest rates of different countries one to another. This was the predominant mechanism prior to 1914. Of course, among the different countries there existed many variations in legal institutions, administrative devices, redemption techniques, conversion practices, and so on. But these were small marginal differences which did not prevent what was, in effect, a viable international monetary mechanism binding together a large part of the world. Somewhat surprisingly, in hindsight, governments interfered directly only occasionally. Money tended to move freely from one market to another, thus tending to equalize interest rates. Domestic price levels in the moderately long run were fairly stable. Movements of labor were less restricted than they are at present. Exchange rates, although not absolutely fixed, varied within a relatively narrow band of fluctuations essentially determined by twice the total cost of shipping gold: the gold export and gold import points of the classical gold standard. Few policing costs were involved; the system was self-supporting. Even the actual shipment of gold to settle international balances was remarkably small compared to the importance of gold in domestic usage as coin or indirectly as monetary reserves against other domestic moneys.

Although nations employed different names for their moneys, such as pounds, marks, dollars, or francs, there really existed a common monetary medium through the conversion of the different moneys into gold, thus promoting the interrelationships of the various economies and the consequent expansion of the division of labor. Such a single money system, tied to a commodity (gold) which itself changed in quantity only slowly, provided a de facto restriction of the total monetary stock of the world. True, some new discoveries of gold fields, or new technical processes such as the cyanide process, at times introduced some sudden expansions. But the overall importance of new current production declined inexorably relative to stocks, as it continues to do to this day. The instability introduced by these discoveries and inventions seems modest indeed compared to that currently being experienced through the use of independent national currencies as reserves, the invention of Special Drawing Rights, and the universal practice of deficit financing—to say nothing of the myriad of discretionary devices and direct controls being practiced by practically all nations, either separately or collectively.

As a result of the adoption of gold coin standards by various countries, there came into being a relatively automatic international balance-of-payments mechanism. Governments (central banks) were not only not necessary or required; by the so-called rules of the games they were undesirable and antithetical. The variation in domestic money stocks was held in check by international gold movements, not by the discretionary actions of national central banks subject to the push and pull of domestic political pressures. The mechanism was not perfect (for what is perfect in human affairs?), but it provided a symmetrical adjustment system functioning internationally with a minimum of conscious guidance, reducing monetary reserves in a country selling gold from its stocks and raising reserves in a country acquiring it; raising short-term interest rates in a country selling its gold stock and lowering them in a country acquiring gold; reducing monetary stocks in a country selling gold and increasing monetary stocks in a country acquiring it; and, ultimately, if it went far enough, lowering price levels in countries selling gold and raising them in countries acquiring it. This, quite clearly, is an equilibrium mechanism. No one should deny it, although it could be argued by some (and has been) that the side effects were too costly by compelling a country to accept a politically unacceptable level of unemployment or some other disciplinary measure.

Obviously, the international gold standard as described above is no more. It was not abandoned all at once, or suddenly, nor did all who abandoned it do so voluntarily or for the same reasons. Perhaps the beginning, the camel's nose under the tent, was the recognition that under a gold coin standard, holders of gold are able to impose some restraint on the discretionary powers governments wish to possess in order to pursue their various political or economic objectives, e.g., export promotion, full employment, faster economic growth, arbitrarily low interest rates, agricultural or other subsidies, forced and rapid industrialization, and so on *ad infinitum*. In terms of American experience (although it applies in general to other countries as well), the deterioration of the gold standard probably began when moneys other than gold were made full legal tender, when ownership of gold was restricted, and when restraints were put upon the export and import of the metal as well as upon contractual arrangements based upon gold. The crucial year in the American experience is 1933-1934. Space does not permit the detailing of the actions taken at that time. Except for gold coins minted before 1934, ownership of the metal in private hands was prohibited; it became a government monopoly. All moneys were declared full legal tender and completely interchangeable one with another; gold contracts were rendered unenforceable. Interestingly enough, the domestic purpose seems to have been inflationary and the assertion by the President of the United States that it "seeks the kind of dollar which a generation hence will have the same purchasing power as the dollar we hope to attain in the near future" sounds like a line from a comic opera.

The United States retained the pretense of redemption in coin at some unspecified future date. The Gold Reserve Act of 1934 devalued the dollar from its previous weight to "15 5/21sts grains of gold, 9/10 fine," thus reducing the pure gold content to 13.714+ and establishing $35 per ounce (480/13.714) as the official gold price in terms of dollars. Other countries either led or followed suit, some sooner, some later. Thus, the deterioration of the international gold standard continued and, the evidence suggests, at an increasing rate. Although the United States retained its ties to gold internationally by a sort of administratively discretionary gold bullion standard, the severing of the ties to gold continued both in the United States and abroad. From that time on, recurring international monetary crises were probably unavoidable.

In 1944 the Bretton Woods Conference, inspired by and executed by representatives of governments and dominated by the United States and Great Britain, formulated an international gold-dollar exchange standard, having most of the disadvantages of a gold standard and few, if any, of its virtues. In essence, nations other than the United States agreed to maintain a relatively fixed rate between their monetary units and the dollar, with the latter redeemable to governments at $35 per ounce. The intent seems to have been to permit more frequent readjustments of the relatively fixed rates than did, in fact, take place. But intentions, however worthy, are well known for their applications in certain road-paving projects.

The system thus established functioned for some years. The very large reserves of gold held by the United States, themselves as much the result of political circumstances (such as the gold outflow from Europe to the United States between Munich in September 1938 and the fall of France in June 1940) as economic, permitted the IMF system to function for many years. Perhaps the reserves, if smaller, would have forced the system to be abandoned much earlier.

In domestic monetary affairs, the Congress proceeded to remove or destroy all the vestigial ties to gold. In 1946 the gold certificate reserve requirement for Federal Reserve Banks was reduced from 40 percent against Federal Reserve notes and 35 percent against Federal Reserve deposits (the basic reserve against deposit liabilities of American member banks) to a single 25 percent against both. In 1960 the prohibition on holding gold domestically by American citizens was expanded to prohibit them from holding gold internationally as well. They were accused of being a part of those ubiquitous speculators who, invariably, are devilishly bent upon causing international monetary crises. The money stock of the United States continued to increase, but not at a constant rate. The gold stock continued to decline, and at what appears to be an increasing rate. Step by step, in the 1960s, the ties were cut. Cash, not gold, of course, was permitted to be counted as member bank reserves for the first time since 1913. Even the minor vestigial remains of silver in the monetary system were abandoned. First, the gold certificate requirement of 25 percent against Federal Reserve deposits was removed, and then the gold certificate reserve against Federal Reserve notes. The present ratio of monetary gold stock to Federal Reserve deposit and note issue liabilities is close to 10 percent, less than one-half the previously lowered ratio specified by law. Had the requirement been maintained, unquestionably that increase in the total money stock of the United States could not have reached its present level. The check-rein had been thrown away.

The international gold-dollar exchange standard agreed upon at Bretton Woods was inhibited for many years by the hangover of blocked accounts and exchange controls remaining from the war. By 1958, however, the various monetary reforms in Europe induced what amounted to full interconvertibility of currencies among the major nations of the Western world. Now the gold-dollar exchange standard was in full swing; it soon demonstrated some of the difficulties that many had previously recognized. There was no adjustment mechanism. Under the more traditional gold standard with national currencies defined in gold and reserves maintained therein, countries could not acquire new reserves except by acquiring gold. Now, however, a country with a surplus in its balance of payments could create new money against its foreign balances (that is, dollars for the most part). Dollar balances in American banks became monetary reserves. Nor was there any pressure on the United States to adjust or terminate the deficit in its balance of payments as there would have been under a true gold standard. Adjustments could have been made through the utilization of appropriate central bank techniques, especially open market operations. But it would be particularly naive to expect it. Moreover, it is clear that this did not happen.

Of course, gold was still in the picture, internationally. Foreign central banks could still demand gold at the official dollar price of $35 per ounce. There was even a "free" gold market or two, the one in London being most important. In October 1961 the London price for gold spurted above $40 per ounce, and in reaction against the usual wicked speculators, a gold pool was formed by the major nations. For some years that pool furnished enough gold to the "free" market to prevent the price from rising very far above the $35 level. Maintaining an effective price ceiling is always a difficult matter; the gold price did not prove to be an exception. In 1968 a major international monetary crisis, sometimes mislabeled a dollar crisis, led to abandoning the gold pool. France had left the sinking ship earlier. In its stead the nations formed a so-called two-tier gold price, one the official $35 per ounce, and the other a price to be determined in the "free" market without intervention from central banks' reserves to influence the price. The next major crisis occurred in August 1971 and resulted in the United States' discontinuing the sale of gold to foreign central banks at the official price, thus casting aside the second generic requirement for a gold standard: the agency prepared to buy and sell gold for money, and money for gold.

The "closing of the gold window" in August 1971 placed the United States and the USSR in a very similar position. Both countries have monetary units defined in terms of gold; neither country has an effective agency prepared to buy and sell at the monetary price. There is no convertibility of the ruble into gold, either domestically or internationally, nor is there any convertibility of the dollar into gold, either domestically or internationally. Both currencies are, in effect, irredeemable paper money, although, to be sure, the dollar is bought, sold, and loaned on the world's markets fairly freely, while the amount of paper rubles or coins bought, sold, or loaned is negligible and such exchanges as do exist are either black market or in the nature of commodity purchase and sale rather than money.

A few months ago, just after the latest crisis in the international money markets, the *Wall Street Journal,* in a thoughtful editorial entitled "Rethinking the Dollar Problem" (March 2, 1973), suggested that the appropriate action called for a tightening of credit by the U.S. Federal Reserve System, thus increasing interest rates here, and for a loosening of credit in Germany, thus lowering interest rates there. This is precisely the mechanics of the first line of adjustment under the gold standard. The adjustment mechanism is virtually automatic instead of requiring the wise decisions of central bankers who have the courage to forego short-run domestic political advantages for the sake of international harmony and well-being. What happens is almost precisely the reverse, as is indicated by the recent attempts of the Reserve authorities to "jawbone" down higher interest rates in the United States—to mention only one inconsistency in American monetary policy.

The international monetary system is still suffering from belief in a mythology stemming, it would appear, from an emotional rather than logical hangover from the depression years of the 1930s when the United States experienced a period of deflation and, concomitantly, a high degree of unemployment. It was the great contribution—or tragedy—of John Maynard Keynes and the Keynesians to have provided an acceptable and plausible theory which seemed to permit nations to proceed their individual ways with their own particular political and ideological programs without regard to their effects on relations among individuals in an increasingly interdependent world. International motives and objectives are always to be subordinate to *the* important objectives of the domestic scene. The solution to unemployment and other structural maladjustments domestically under the Keynesian prescription was to ensure that wage rates in monetary terms were rigid in a downward direction, while engaging in domestic monetary policies designed to inflate the economy sufficiently to bring about a downward movement in real wage rates. If such a prescription is valid for domestic structural imbalances, then, similarly, the imbalances of the international scene can be remedied by international inflation, or to use the appropriate phrase, by the necessary increases in international liquidity.

Perhaps this explanation is an oversimplification, but the essence of it remains valid. Coupled with the use of national currencies as international reserves, particularly the dollar under the gold-dollar exchange standard, it gave rise to the rather schizoid position that continuous American deficits were essential lest international liquidity be threatened. However, the continuation of deficits in the American balance of payments would lead, almost inexorably, to a lack of confidence in the dollar as a stable currency, and to the willingness and ability of the United States to maintain even the international convertibility of the dollar into gold at a fixed price.

This gave rise to the long pressure for some mechanism or solution which would continually increase international liquidity—the creation of paper gold. The most vigorous and active proponent of this solution among academic economists was Professor Robert Triffin. In justice to Triffin's approach, he seemed less concerned about the overall shortage of international liquidity than what he regarded as the irrational, haphazard, absurd nature of the sources of that liquidity in the balance-of-payments deficits of key currency countries. The intellectual debt of this position to Keynes' arguments is well known. In 1943 Keynes argued for *creation* of international currency "capable of *deliberate* expansion and contraction to offset deflationary and inflationary tendencies in effective world demand [italics added]."

There is no demonstrable relation between the volume of world trade and international reserves or, for that matter, between the volume of domestic trade and the volume of domestic reserves or money stock. But, with the exception of a few economists whose voices were raised against the acceptance of the liquidity shortage mythology, much of the subsequent argument was not over the basic question, but rather over the method of creating the international liquidity.[3] Thus we find this sort of statement, or its equivalent, in book after book, treatise after treatise:

> SDRs, therefore, are likely to provide, in the long run, the most lasting and constructive form of help within the international monetary system. . . . They are likely to provide a lasting addition to the world's supply of international money. . . . But by increasing the overall level of international reserves, it should give countries in difficulties a little more elbow-room to solve their problems, whether by financing a balance of payments deficit until domestic measures have time to work, or just by fending off a speculative attack with a larger pile of reserves.[4]

The point here is less a criticism of the authors than an attempt to show how the acceptance of the liquidity problem focused attention on the shadow rather than the substance.

The substance is the question of the nature of the adjustment mechanism; even accepting the Keynesian statement cited above, what are the rules to be followed for the "deliberate" (by whom?) expansions and contractions? And what incentives and disincentives can be devised to be sure that the exercise of such "deliberate" expansions and contractions will not, even with the best intentions, contract when they should expand, or expand when they should contract? Indeed, liquidity was not the problem; or, if it was, the problem was too much liquidity rather than too little. Even the much heralded SDRs have simply added to the problem. Countries receiving allocations of SDRs can, if they wish, monetize these domestically. If the United States chose to do so, the effects of the SDRs could be made precisely the same as if there had been an inflow of gold. Nor is this problem confined to the United States. Hence, if the SDRs have any effect, it is likely to be in the direction of foreign central banks substituting SDRs for dollars in their international reserves portfolio. At worst, SDRs will contribute to the severity of the ensuing crises; at best the effect will be negligible.

One must point out that the devaluation of the dollar, in accordance with the Smithsonian Agreement of December 1971, also increases liquidity. So does the devaluation of February 1973. If the United States proposed to monetize the increases in the price of gold from $35 to $38 to $42.22, it would have the same effect as if there had been an inflow of gold. This is an adjustment mechanism? On the contrary, it is a maladjustment mechanism, a thermometer that registers lower when it is hot and higher when it is cold. If this argument is correct, we are proposing solutions to the problem by advocating larger doses of the drug that caused the problem in the first place.

International monetary crises are recurring at shorter and shorter intervals and are becoming increasingly severe. Generally, Western nations have done little, if anything, to liberalize overall trade policies and, instead, have turned increasingly to direct controls on trade, capital investment, and even monetary movements. If anything resembling the present system is to survive, it will have to be accompanied by elimination of such controls, not by their imposition. If national objectives are always to have higher priority than international balance and worldwide integration, the present system cannot survive. Nor, indeed, is there the likelihood of conscious adoption of a true gold standard viable over an extended period of time, no matter how much some of us might like to see it.

I have long been a vigorous proponent of a full gold coin standard, although I am quite prepared to admit that it is not perfect, not a panacea. Nor indeed is any of the other proposals thus far. Over a decade ago I expressed the following hope:

> The gold standard is not a perfectly marvelous solution to all our problems. But it is a step in the right direction and even retaining the present [1962] more or less weak links to gold may someday allow us to take further steps. When the severe run on gold took place in 1960, when the next run on gold takes place, as it is quite likely to do, these will still serve as a signal and, if the signal flashes long enough and bright enough, perhaps the United States —government and electorate alike—will come to recognize its meaning and to consider seriously a solution. People are not best served in a free society by granting special powers to administrative agents, whether in monetary or other affairs. Discretion in monetary affairs ought to be reduced, ought to be freed from political influences both domestic and foreign, ought to be minimized and ultimately eliminated. A gold coin standard will, if properly augmented, go far toward achieving that objective.[5]

I am far more pessimistic now. The signals have flashed again and again without, regrettably, any serious decision having been reached. The present monetary system of the Western world is a system of perpetual inflation. All the ties to gold on which a reasonable gold standard solution might have been reached have been cut. Even if we took the simple route of so increasing the official price of gold that the price could absorb all the monetary overhang, and then reinstating an international gold standard, this could only be brought about by conscious planning by various governments, with all the maneuvering for advantages, domestic pressures, and international prestige that this would entail. The gold standard was a discovery, an evolutionary happening, not a conscious innovation. If a gold standard or its equivalent, perhaps in a form as yet unknown, could again become a reality, it could occur only after a prolonged period of time in which the freely operating market forces could establish stable market prices for gold and indicate the proper mint pars for different national monetary units, tied once again by conversion into gold. It would certainly require terminating most of the present prohibitions on the ownership of gold and of foreign currencies or accounts—and perhaps the abolition of government stockpiles of gold as well. At least two preliminary steps to a true gold standard would appear to be: (1) to remove all governmental restraints on the possession, purchase, sale, export, or import of gold in any form, and all restrictions on private contracts involving a quantitative gold payment; (2) to allow for a period of time during which the exchange rates among the major nations of the world would be permitted to seek stable equilibrium levels without dirty floats, devaluations, or governmental support or hindrance of any kind.

Some friends and colleagues may jump to the conclusion that, after years of steadfastly advocating a gold standard, I have become a positive proponent of freely flexible exchange rates. Not so. I remain unconvinced that the three-legged stool of freely flexible exchange rates, locked-in rates of change in the domestic money supply, and the elimination of discretionary monetary authority domestically is either inherently a better system than a gold standard or more likely to prevail over a long period. Rather, I should hope that these two preliminary steps would result in the adoption of a true gold coin standard, if only in one country. Perhaps its success would encourage others to do the same until there would result a renewal of progress toward a free international society, with a greater stability and a greater degree of international division of labor, a greater prosperity, and a greater stimulus to the individual human spirit than the world has yet seen.

To prescribe the essential preliminary steps is less foolhardy than to predict that they will be taken, although stranger things have happened. In the long run, considering the upward progress man has made compared to his simian ancestors, I am reasonably optimistic, although the process may take a century or two. In the shorter run I am realistically pessimistic. Is the gold standard gone forever? I don't know for sure. Forever is a very long time.

NOTES

[1]This was the result of the statute of 1834 which provided for a 10-percent alloy instead of the prior 1/12ths, and of the codification of 1873, repeated again in the Gold Standard Act of 1900. I omit references to the bimetallic standard.

[2]Houghton-Mifflin Economics/Business News, Spring 1973, p. 8.

[3]See, for example, the discussion in Triffin, *Our International Monetary System: Yesterday, Today and Tomorrow* (New York: Random House, College Division, 1968), pp. 119-124.

[4]William M. Clarke and George Pulay, *The World's Money* (New York: Praeger, 1971), p. 70.

[5]*The Role of Gold* (Washington, D.C.: American Enterprise Association, Public Policy Studies, 1963), p. 79.

Epilogue

It is not money, as is sometimes said, but the destruction of money through inflation that is the root of many evils. Since these chapters were written, in the spring of 1973, the global inflation has accelerated its monetary destruction and thereby evoked more ominous economic, social, political, and moral consequences. In most parts of the world the annual depreciation rates of the national monetary units now exceed 10 percent and are rising steadily. Even in the United States the overall cost of living data as issued by the federal government is rising breathlessly at two-digit rates. Inflation of such force is corrosive to the social fabric of society; it becomes the great destroyer of the social order.

And yet, there is no foreseeable end to the monetary destruction as the ideological and political forces that are giving rise to such destructive policies continue to gain strength and support. Most people and their elected representatives and officials in high government offices do not understand the inflation dilemma. They are searching in vain for solutions in political courage and integrity and more government control. But in the fog of confusion and ignorance even the most determined statesman, if he were to emerge, could not find his way to safety. Nothing can stop inflation until the redistributive society learns to exert discipline and moderation and the economic gospel of Keynesianism that is dominating public education is forever discredited.

In the darkness of economic ignorance inflation ravages the

middle class and destroys the social order. Gold, which has been man's money throughout the ages, is an important barometer of this destruction. As gold investors we may rejoice about the soaring gold price, but as members of a highly productive society we are fearful of the ominous consequences of the paper money depreciation, which the rising gold price so distinctly reveals. Rampant inflation not only impedes social cooperation and division of labor, but also breeds massive unemployment and deep depression. The economic disruption it causes, together with its radical redistribution of wealth and income, lead to social upheaval, lawlessness, and deprivation. Ugly strikes may paralyze economic life, bloody riots may cripple the cities and disrupt the distribution of essential goods. As it becomes impoverished and embittered by inflation, the middle class may clamor for law and order, food and jobs, and return to normalcy by force, if necessary. It may welcome "strong leaders" with emergency powers over prices, wages, rents, and many other aspects of economic life in order to restore economic and social order. But unfortunately, strong governments can only suppress certain disorders; they cannot restore the marvelous market order that can only spring from individual freedom.

In spite of their great popularity, governmental controls over prices do not alleviate the inflation dilemma. On the contrary, they seriously hamper economic production, create shortages of vital goods and services, breed black markets, and above all, create confusion and disorder whenever and wherever they are applied. They merely constitute attempts at elevating political might over economic law; and their inevitable failures again and again offer cogent proof of the futility of such attempts.

The lowly U.S. penny offers an example of this failure. It is about to become worth more as a piece of copper than as a U.S. coin. Like all silver coins before it, the penny, too, will soon disappear from circulation, hiding from inflation. Therefore, in blindness and desperation the men of the U.S. Treasury have imposed a ban on melting and exporting copper pennies, under penalty of $10,000 fine and five years imprisonment. No one could possibly offer a more befitting testimony of the intellectual and moral bankruptcy of the fiat money order.

While the international monetary system is disintegrating thousands of barter arrangements throughout the world are taking the place of monetary exchanges. Universal lack of confidence in paper currency is hampering foreign trade and precipitating a worldwide depression. For the first time in its twenty-eight-year history the United Nations' opening session, in April 1974, dealt with monetary and economic problems. The Secretary-General declared a global emergency caused by the breakdown of the world monetary system.

And yet, in these dark hours of monetary night the early light of a new day is clearly visible. In order to avoid further economic disintegration and retreat into barter, some central banks can be expected to resume gold payments among each other. They may return to a quasi gold-exchange standard that facilitates international exchanges through payment of gold. Certainly no return to fixed parities between gold and national currencies can be expected at this time; all we can expect is a parallel standard that utilizes both gold and paper currencies at market exchange rates. But such a system would be a modest beginning of a new order that would again afford central banks a choice between gold and fiat money. We are confident that gold will once again emerge as the most favored medium of exchange, the money of the world.

In America the early light of a new day became visible when on August 15, 1974, President Ford signed a bill that on January 1, 1975 restored the individual freedom to trade and hold gold. This freedom to own the precious metal does not, however, encompass the individual freedom to use gold in economic exchanges. The U.S. Treasury now claims that the Gold Clause Joint Resolution (31 U.S.C. 463), which Congress passed on June 5, 1933, denies Americans the right to make payment in gold or a particular kind of coin or currency. Only government paper issued by the Federal Reserve System or the U.S. Treasury is the current legal tender.

The authors deplore this denial of monetary freedom and, therefore, hope that all legal tender laws that afford paper money a monopolistic position in all payments, public and private, will be repealed, or at least amended to permit "gold contracts" and "gold clauses." Once again, the American people must be free to make contracts in terms of gold. But we seriously doubt that the American people will soon regain this right to gold as money. After all, the redistributive society cannot tolerate monetary freedom. Its monetary tools are central banks and fiat money, legal tender legislation and currency regulation, inflation and price controls. Its destination is hyperinflation and chaos.

HFS
Grove City College, Pa.
January 1, 1975

Index

201